D0581880

# When One
### is
# Expecting

FROM THE CREATOR OF
@pippatips

# When One is Expecting

## A POSH PERSON'S GUIDE TO PREGNANCY AND PARENTING

ICON

Published in the UK in 2013 by
Icon Books Ltd, Omnibus Business Centre,
39–41 North Road, London N7 9DP
email: info@iconbooks.net
www.iconbooks.net

Sold in the UK, Europe and Asia
by Faber & Faber Ltd, Bloomsbury House,
74-77 Great Russell Street,
London WC1B 3DA or their agents

Distributed in the UK, Europe and Asia
by TBS Ltd, TBS Distribution Centre,
Colchester Road, Frating Green,
Colchester CO7 7DW

Distributed in Australia and New
Zealand by Allen & Unwin Pty Ltd,
PO Box 8500, 83 Alexander Street,
Crows Nest, NSW 2065

Distributed in Canada by Penguin Books
Canada, 90 Eglinton Avenue East,
Suite 700, Toronto, Ontario M4P 2YE

Distributed in India by Penguin Books
India, 11 Community Centre,
Panchsheel Park, New Delhi 110017

Distributed in South Africa by Book
Promotions, Office B4, The District,
41 Sir Lowry Road, Woodstock 7925

ISBN: 978-1-84831-641-6

Text copyright © Mat Morrisroe and
Suzanne Azzopardi, 2013

The authors have asserted their
moral rights.

The picture acknowledgements on
p272 constitute an extension of this
copyright page.

The advice in this book has been
produced as a parody, and should not
be taken seriously. This is not intended as
a guide to child-rearing. The characters in
this book are fictional. Any resemblance
to any persons, living or dead, is entirely
coincidental.

No part of this book may be reproduced in
any form, or by any means, without prior
permission in writing from the publisher.

Typeset by seagulls.net

Printed and bound in the UK by CPI Group
(UK) Ltd, Croydon, CR0 4YY

*To all the Mamas and Papas out there for inspiring me, and all the other great bands from the Sixties that I listened to while waiting for my ghost-writers to finish this book*

# Introduction

# Introduction

*Apart from deciding which hat to wear to Ascot, whether or not to have a child is one of the biggest decisions a person can make. There is nothing quite so rewarding as that first smile, that first step or that first off-piste run at Klosters.*

*Pregnancy is one of the most popular methods of breeding humans, but I know that having a baby is about far more than just giving birth.*

*So whether you want to find out which brand of champagne is best for baby, which art director to use for your in-utero portraits, or which names look best with 'Lord' or 'Lady' in front of them, this book is for you. In fact, most people were babies once so this book is for everybody.*

*Full of tips and wisdom to help you through the coming travails, it will help you be prepared for every challenge that having a little one in your life can throw at you. Think of it as your mentor, your guide, your baby consultant\* – giving you and your child the best head start one can have.*

\* Of course, I don't know everything about babies, so very occasionally you may be better placed speaking with a medical professional, interior designer, pâtissier, stylist or team of psychologists.

# Reasons for having a baby

- *You have great ideas for baby names*

- *You enjoyed playing with dolls or action figures as a child*

- *You need to produce an heir to solve an inheritance or succession crisis*

- *You are competing with friends*

- *You are looking to launch your career as a 'Mumpreneur'*

- *You are looking for ideas for your column, book or reality TV show*

- *Your pooch is getting on a bit*

- *You have too much spare time/money*

- *You have a spare room that needs brightening up*

- *You want a reason to plan events and parties for the years to come*

- *You would like to make Mother's Day more 'me focused'*

- *You started life as a baby*

- *You want to have a baby*

- *Love*

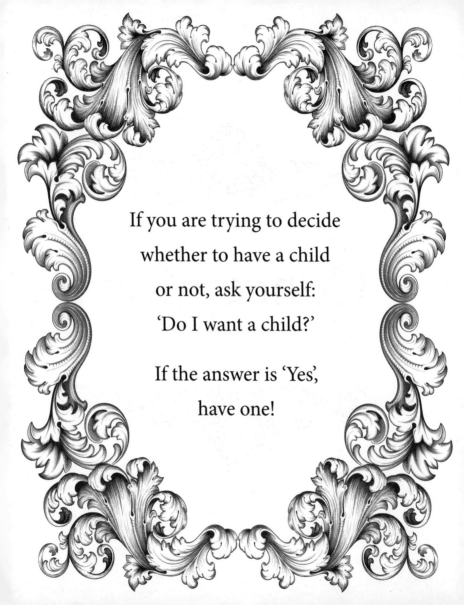

If you are trying to decide whether to have a child or not, ask yourself: 'Do I want a child?'

If the answer is 'Yes', have one!

# Conception

In days gone by, babies were delivered by storks or left in cabbage patches. However, these traditional methods have now been almost totally supplanted by a woman growing a baby human in her 'womb'.

There are many ways for this to occur, but the most statistically popular is having 'sex'.

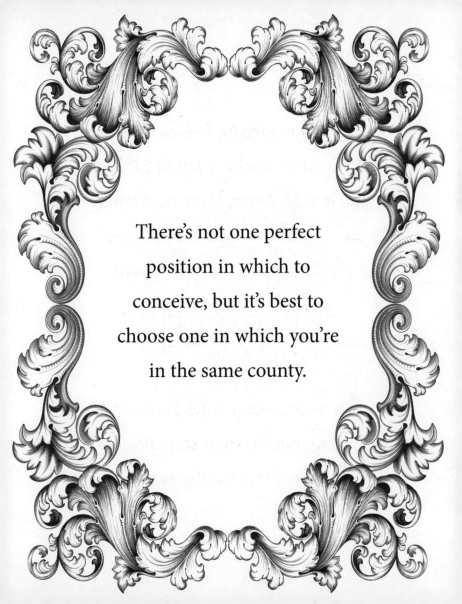

There's not one perfect position in which to conceive, but it's best to choose one in which you're in the same county.

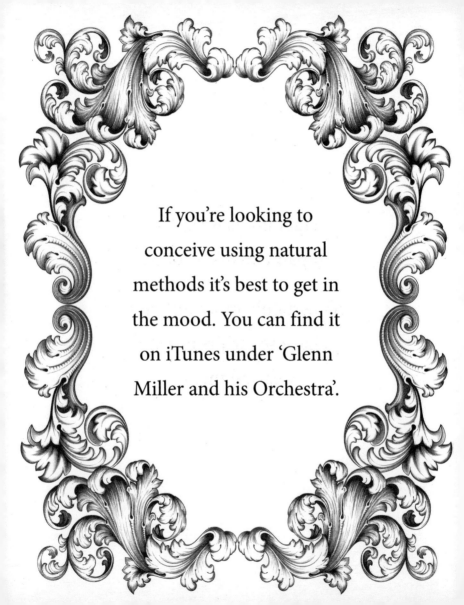

If you're looking to conceive using natural methods it's best to get in the mood. You can find it on iTunes under 'Glenn Miller and his Orchestra'.

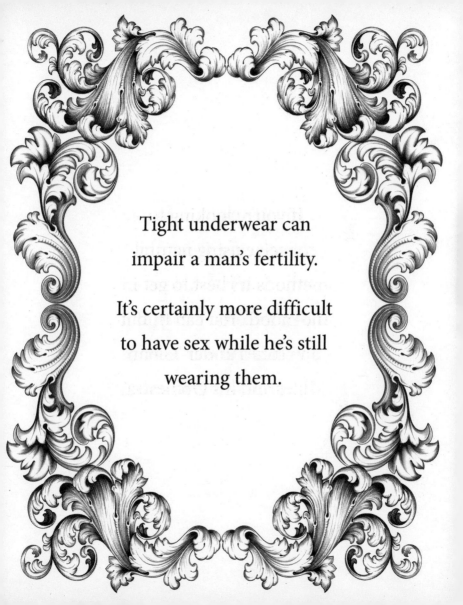

Tight underwear can impair a man's fertility.

It's certainly more difficult to have sex while he's still wearing them.

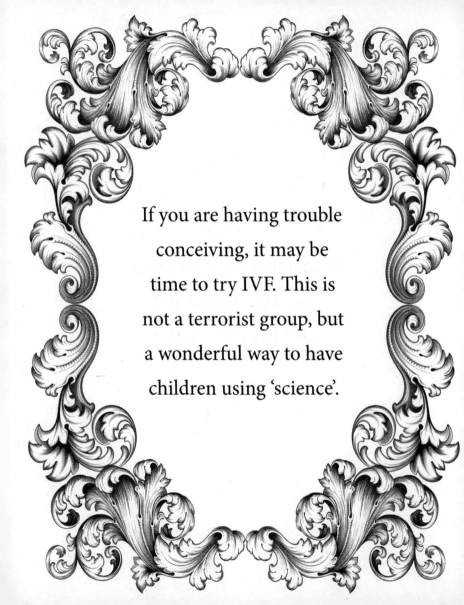

If you are having trouble conceiving, it may be time to try IVF. This is not a terrorist group, but a wonderful way to have children using 'science'.

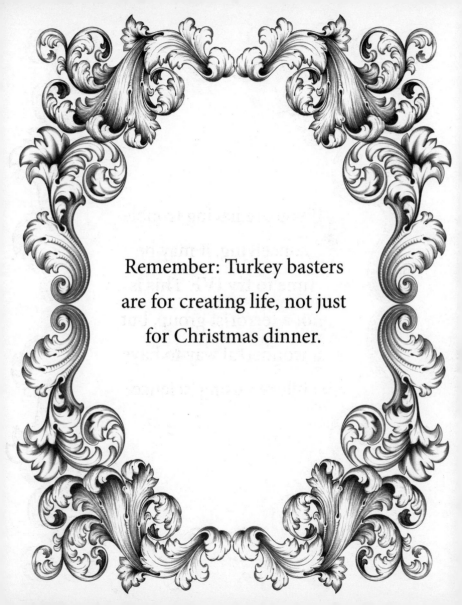

Remember: Turkey basters are for creating life, not just for Christmas dinner.

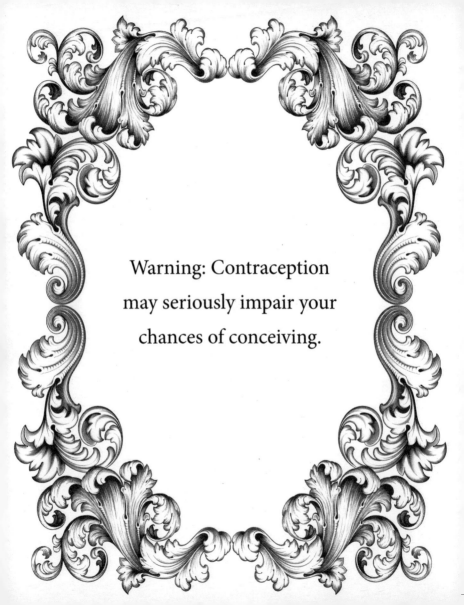

Warning: Contraception
may seriously impair your
chances of conceiving.

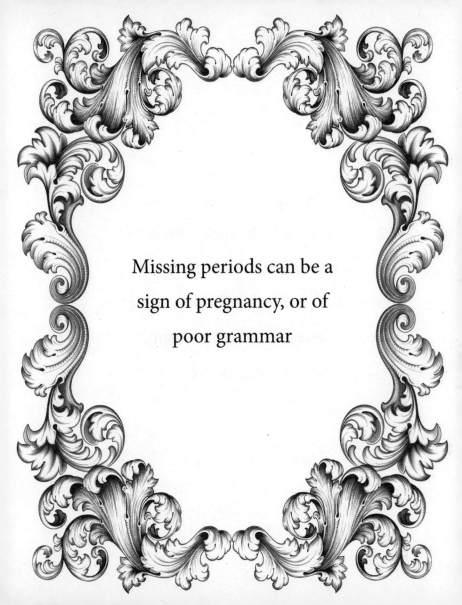

Missing periods can be a sign of pregnancy, or of poor grammar

If the stick shows two blue lines then you're almost definitely pregnant. If it shows a circle with a diagonal line through it, you've urinated on your iPod nano.

# *Am I pregnant?*

*Giving birth without knowing you're pregnant limits the options for baby showers, scan parties and the production of a high-quality birth video, so keep an eye out for these tell-tale signs:*

- ❧ *weight gain*
- ❧ *sensitive breasts*
- ❧ *increased appetite and/or cravings for food*
- ❧ *improved sense of smell*
- ❧ *positive pregnancy tests*
- ❧ *large stomach bump*
- ❧ *contractions*
- ❧ *a baby coming out of you*

# The First Trimester: Just Pregnant

*Congratulations! You've made a baby!*

*You may not be ready to announce straight away, so avoid letting people know you're pregnant by not mentioning it.*

*This can be a good moment to contact the professionals, though, so do remember to let your doctor and PR person know.*

At 2 weeks your baby
is the size of a flake of
organic sea salt.

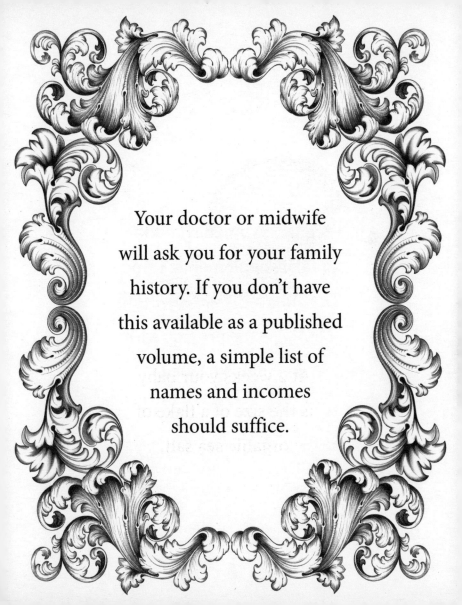

Your doctor or midwife
will ask you for your family
history. If you don't have
this available as a published
volume, a simple list of
names and incomes
should suffice.

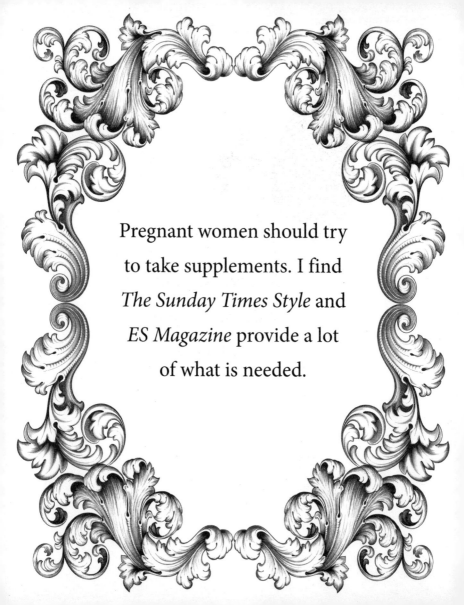

Pregnant women should try to take supplements. I find *The Sunday Times Style* and *ES Magazine* provide a lot of what is needed.

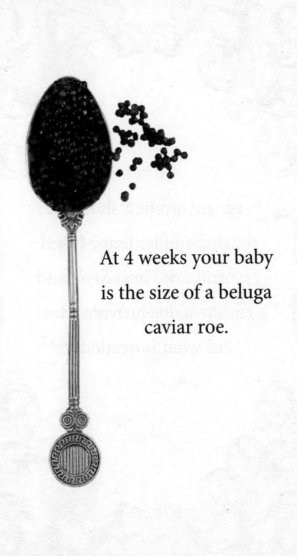

At 4 weeks your baby
is the size of a beluga
caviar roe.

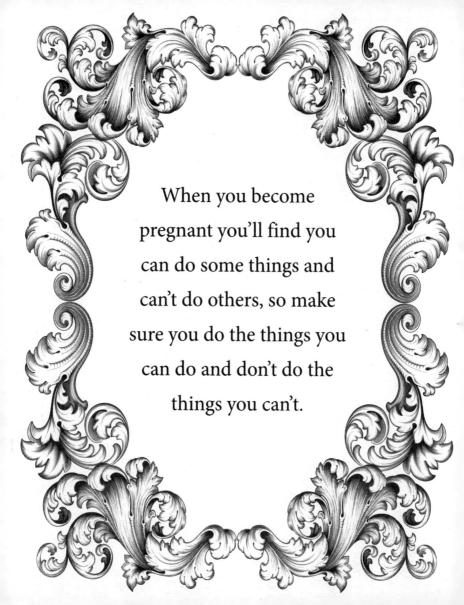

When you become pregnant you'll find you can do some things and can't do others, so make sure you do the things you can do and don't do the things you can't.

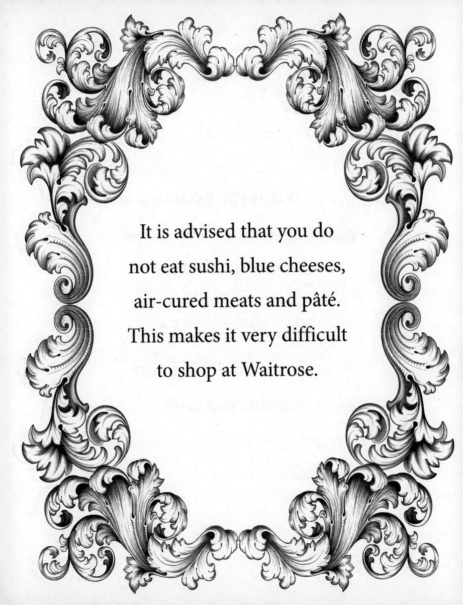

It is advised that you do
not eat sushi, blue cheeses,
air-cured meats and pâté.
This makes it very difficult
to shop at Waitrose.

*Social engagements are rife with problems for the newly pregnant lady, but it's possible to avoid drinking and smoking while staying 'mum':*

✖ *Make people think you're still drinking by having tonic water with ice and lemon or serving it in a martini glass with an olive.*

✖ *Throw people off the scent by cutting a waterproof plaster into a circle and pretending it's a nicotine patch.*

*If you still need some handy excuses to explain why you're not eating or drinking certain things, why not try these:*

❧ *'This shellfish isn't sustainably sourced'*

❧ *'I prefer PETA-approved foie gras'*

❧ *'Thank you no, I'm eating at the palace later'*

❧ *'I'm hungover'*

At 6 weeks your
baby is the size of
a Puy lentil.

Make morning sickness
bearable by thinking of it
as a 'baby hangover'.

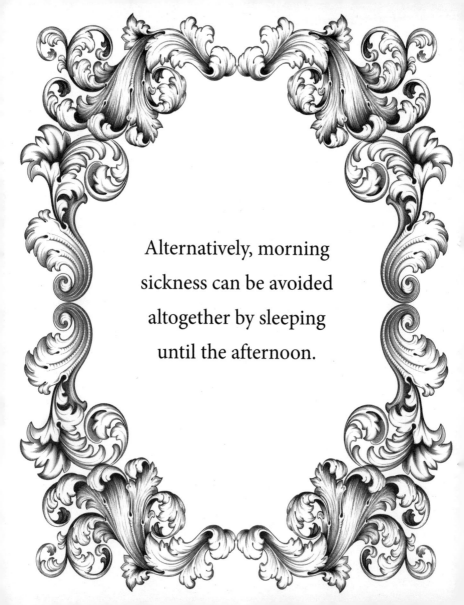

Alternatively, morning sickness can be avoided altogether by sleeping until the afternoon.

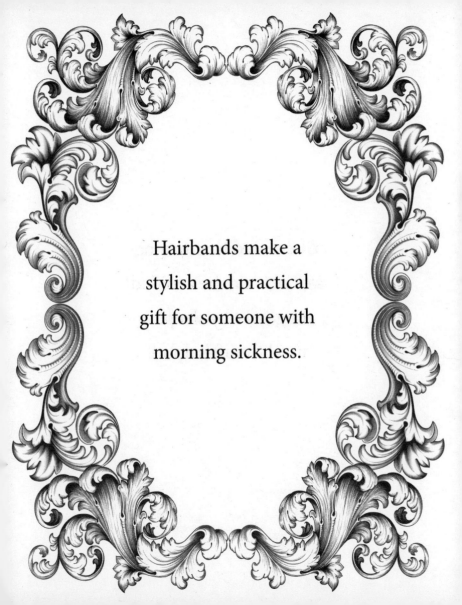

Hairbands make a
stylish and practical
gift for someone with
morning sickness.

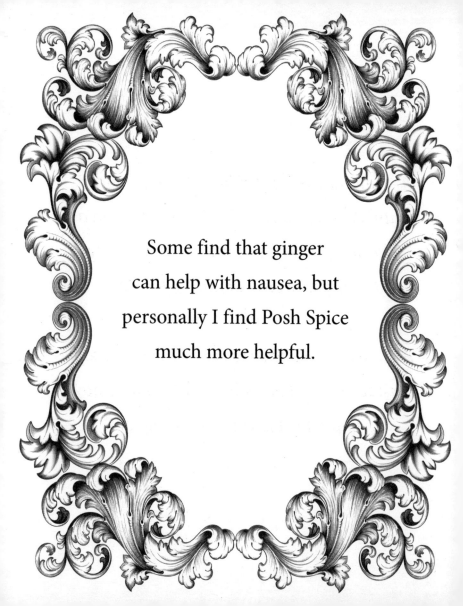

Some find that ginger
can help with nausea, but
personally I find Posh Spice
much more helpful.

*You may have cravings and feel more hungry than usual. This is often known as 'eating for two', but if you were having twins you would be eating for three.*

*A simple rule is to take the number of people inside you and add one (you). That is how many people you are eating for.*

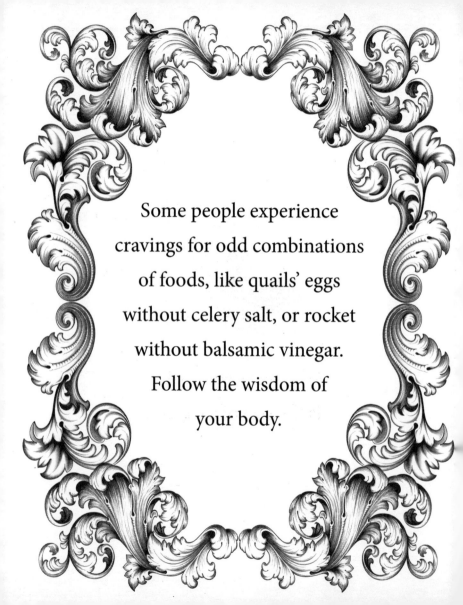

Some people experience cravings for odd combinations of foods, like quails' eggs without celery salt, or rocket without balsamic vinegar. Follow the wisdom of your body.

At 7 weeks your baby
is the size of a caper.

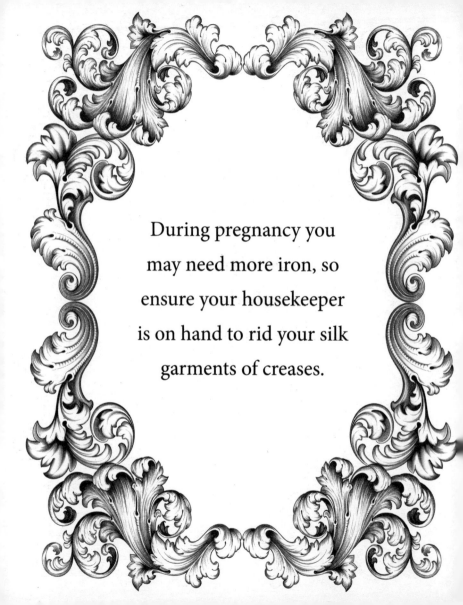

During pregnancy you may need more iron, so ensure your housekeeper is on hand to rid your silk garments of creases.

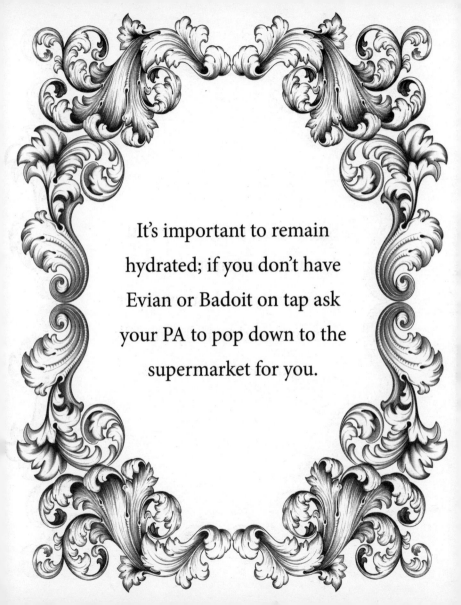

It's important to remain hydrated; if you don't have Evian or Badoit on tap ask your PA to pop down to the supermarket for you.

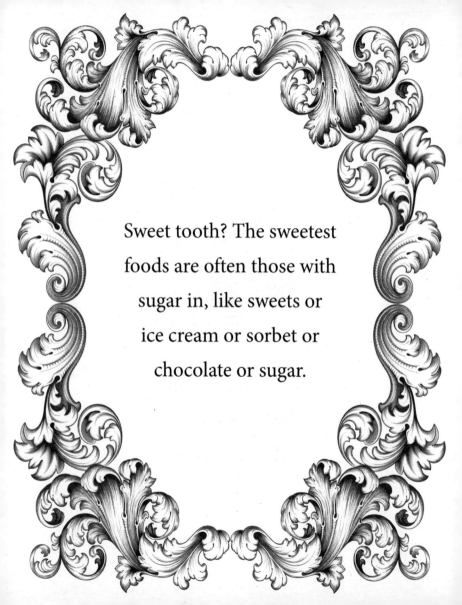

Sweet tooth? The sweetest
foods are often those with
sugar in, like sweets or
ice cream or sorbet or
chocolate or sugar.

At 8 weeks your
baby is the size of an
edamame bean.

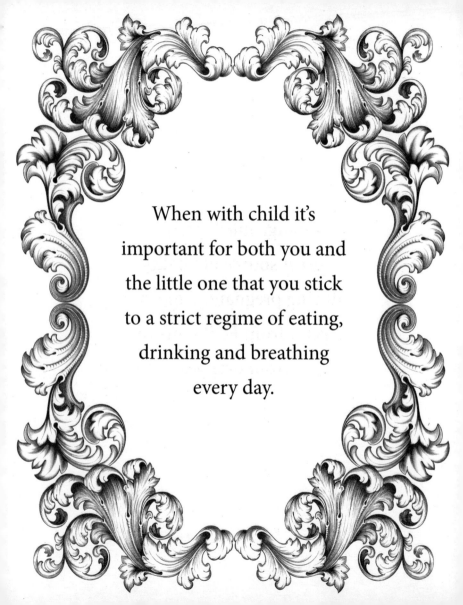

When with child it's important for both you and the little one that you stick to a strict regime of eating, drinking and breathing every day.

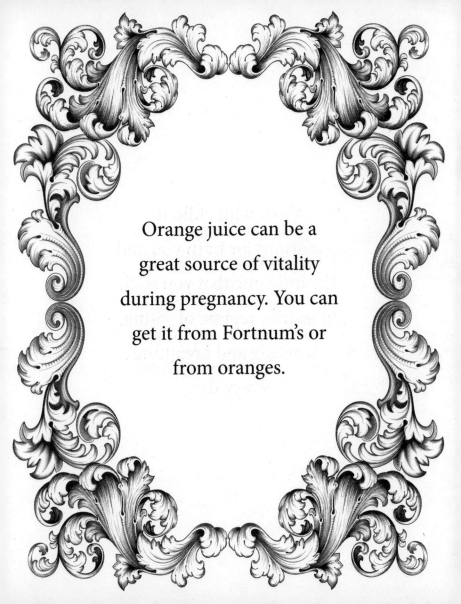

Orange juice can be a great source of vitality during pregnancy. You can get it from Fortnum's or from oranges.

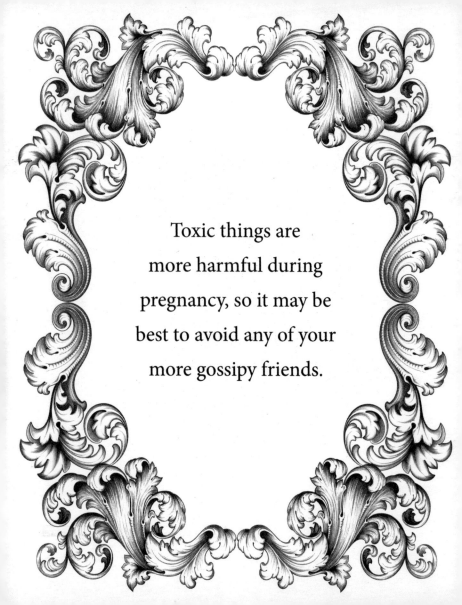

Toxic things are more harmful during pregnancy, so it may be best to avoid any of your more gossipy friends.

At 9 weeks your baby
is the size of a large
sloe berry.

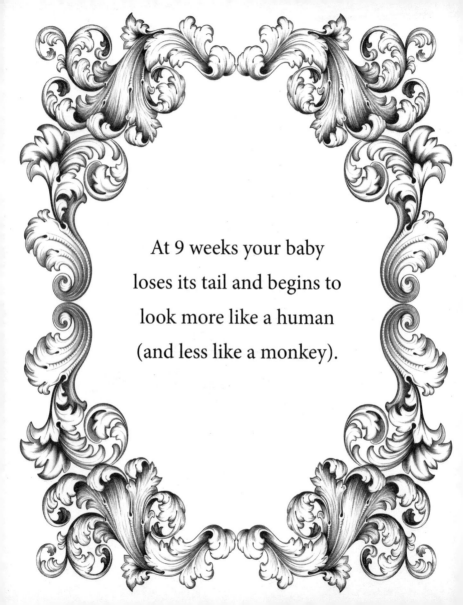

At 9 weeks your baby loses its tail and begins to look more like a human (and less like a monkey).

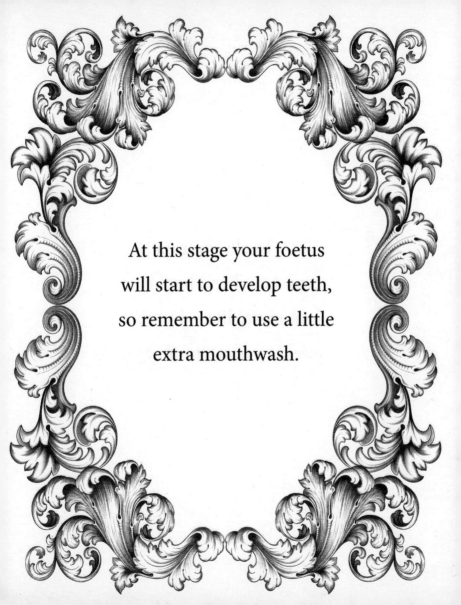

At this stage your foetus
will start to develop teeth,
so remember to use a little
extra mouthwash.

A little heart develops and will beat very quickly: around 140 beats per minute, or *molto allegro*.

At this stage, your baby will begin to frown. Don't worry, it's usually not a reflection on you.

At 10 weeks your
baby is the size of
a quail egg.

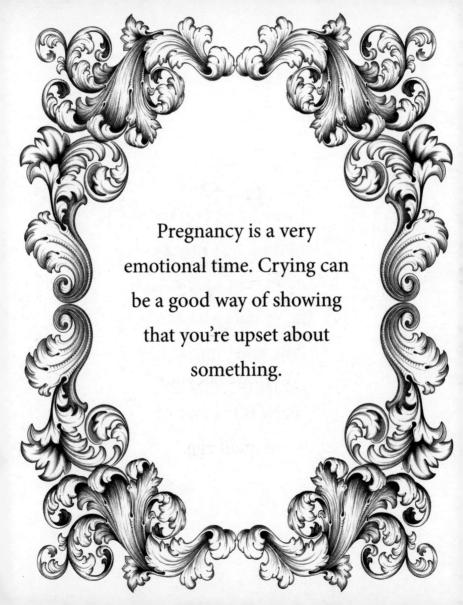

Pregnancy is a very emotional time. Crying can be a good way of showing that you're upset about something.

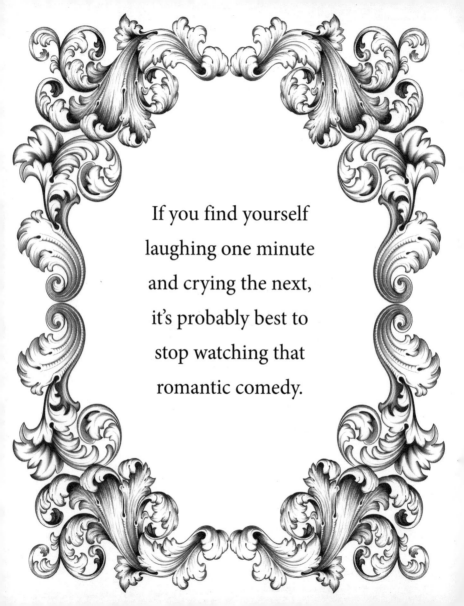

If you find yourself laughing one minute and crying the next, it's probably best to stop watching that romantic comedy.

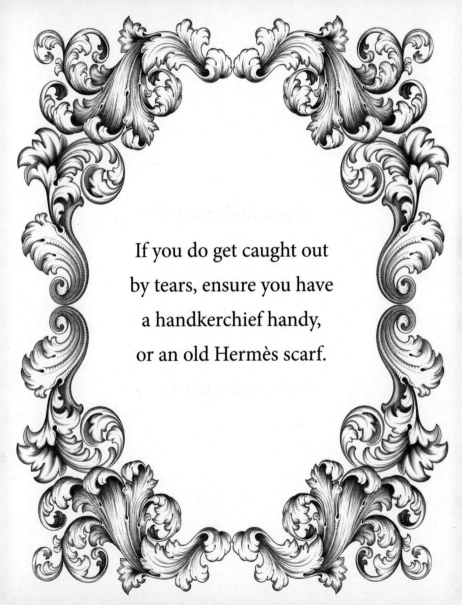

If you do get caught out
by tears, ensure you have
a handkerchief handy,
or an old Hermès scarf.

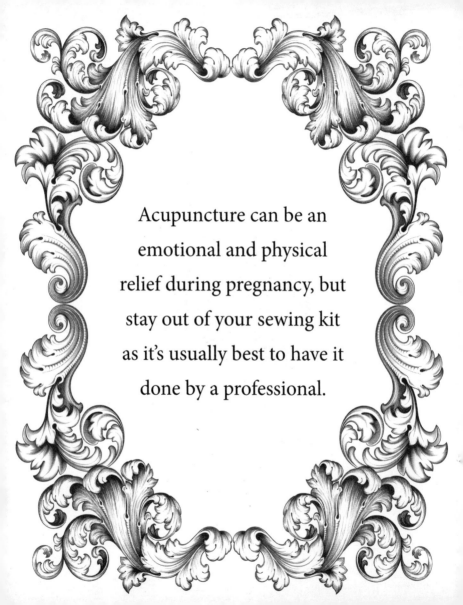

Acupuncture can be an emotional and physical relief during pregnancy, but stay out of your sewing kit as it's usually best to have it done by a professional.

At 11 weeks your baby is

the size of a fresh fig.

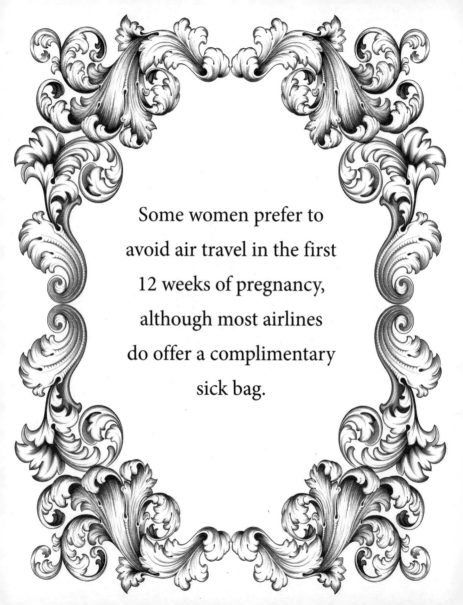

Some women prefer to avoid air travel in the first 12 weeks of pregnancy, although most airlines do offer a complimentary sick bag.

By this time your baby has fingerprints (though they won't be on record at the local police station).

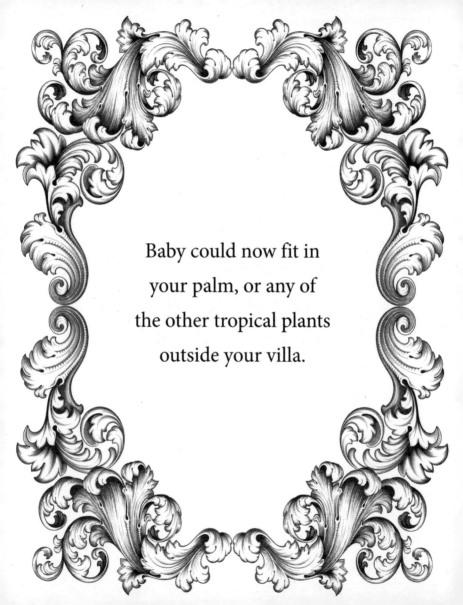

Baby could now fit in your palm, or any of the other tropical plants outside your villa.

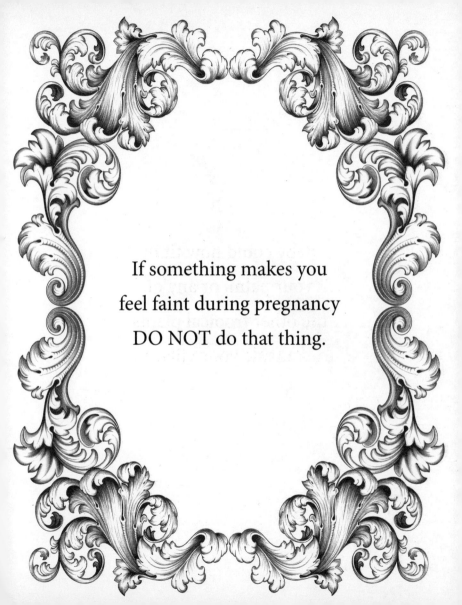

If something makes you
feel faint during pregnancy
DO NOT do that thing.

At 12 weeks your
baby is the size of a
custard apple.

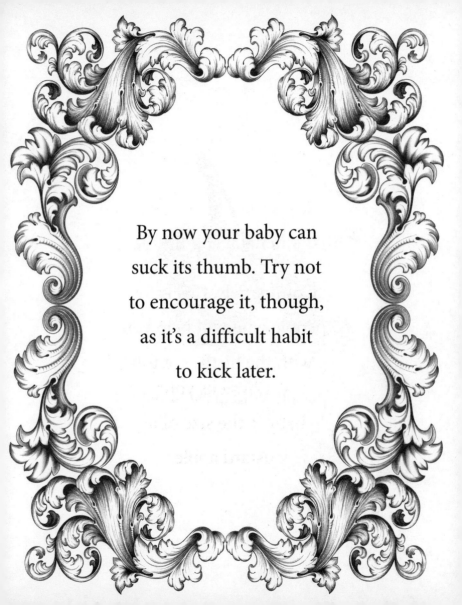

By now your baby can suck its thumb. Try not to encourage it, though, as it's a difficult habit to kick later.

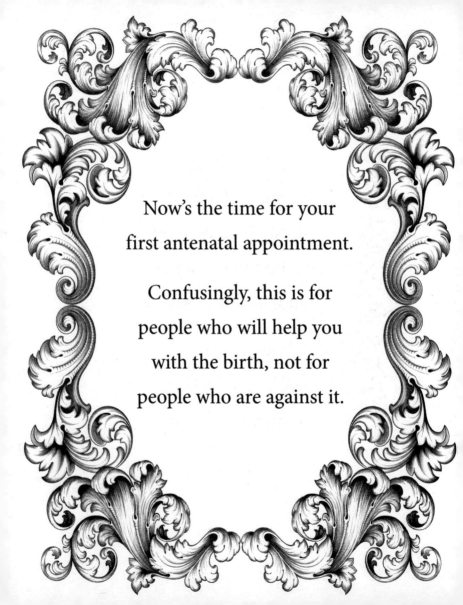

Now's the time for your first antenatal appointment.

Confusingly, this is for people who will help you with the birth, not for people who are against it.

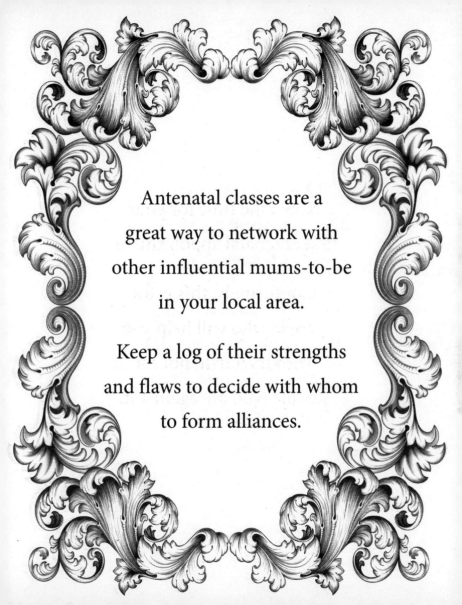

Antenatal classes are a
great way to network with
other influential mums-to-be
in your local area.

Keep a log of their strengths
and flaws to decide with whom
to form alliances.

12 weeks is the perfect time to go for your 12-week scan.

Visit your local hospital for this – nipping through the airport scanner on the way to Mustique won't do the trick.

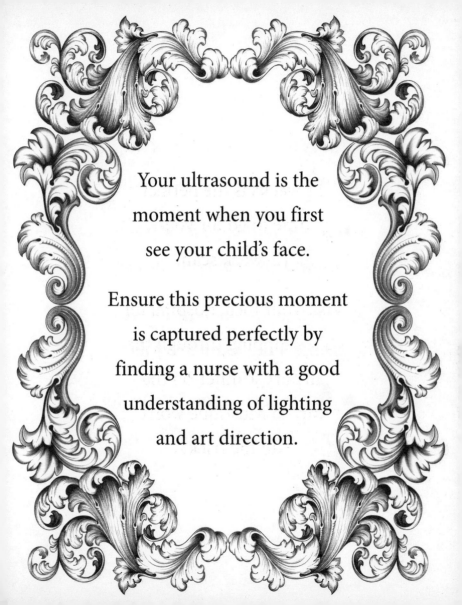

Your ultrasound is the moment when you first see your child's face.

Ensure this precious moment is captured perfectly by finding a nurse with a good understanding of lighting and art direction.

*Think about the way you want people to see your unborn child:*

🎗 *Try a landscape view from a distance for a panoramic feel.*

🎗 *4D close ups are probably better for the more attractive babies.*

🎗 *Soft focus is a good option for foetuses that haven't quite grown into their looks.*

# The Second Trimester: A Growing Middle

*If you would like people to know you are pregnant at this stage – tell them!*

*If you want to write to someone about your pregnancy there's no need to delay the news by posting a letter or sending a carrier dove; simply send an e-mail using a computer.*

*Another good opportunity to announce would be at a large gathering of friends. How about at someone's wedding reception? Combine the news with your toast to the happy couple!*

At 13 weeks your
baby is the size of a
duck egg.

During the second trimester you may begin to suffer from swollen feet or ankles, but the worst side effect of this (i.e. people seeing them) can be avoided by wearing boots.

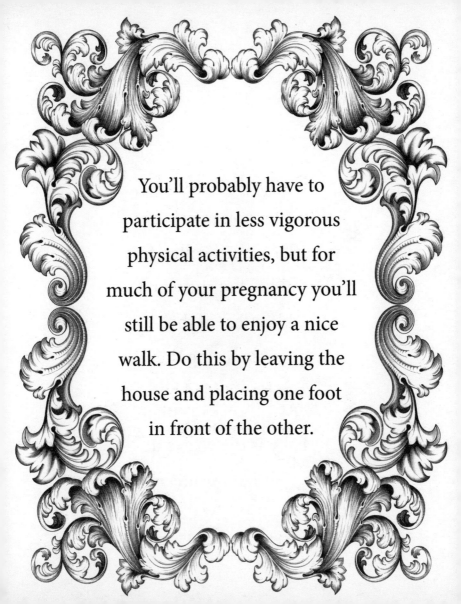

You'll probably have to participate in less vigorous physical activities, but for much of your pregnancy you'll still be able to enjoy a nice walk. Do this by leaving the house and placing one foot in front of the other.

At 14 weeks your
baby is the size of a
dragon fruit.

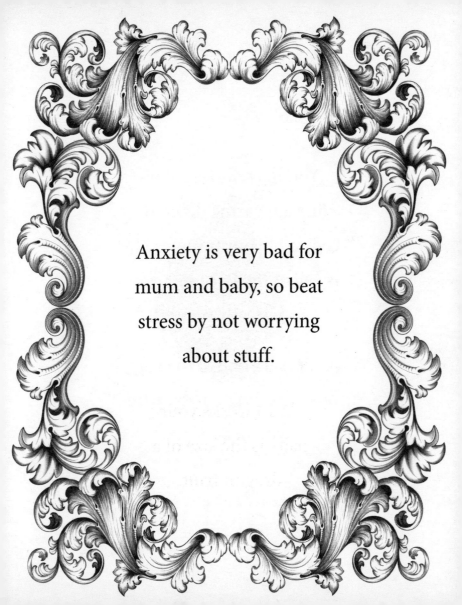

Anxiety is very bad for mum and baby, so beat stress by not worrying about stuff.

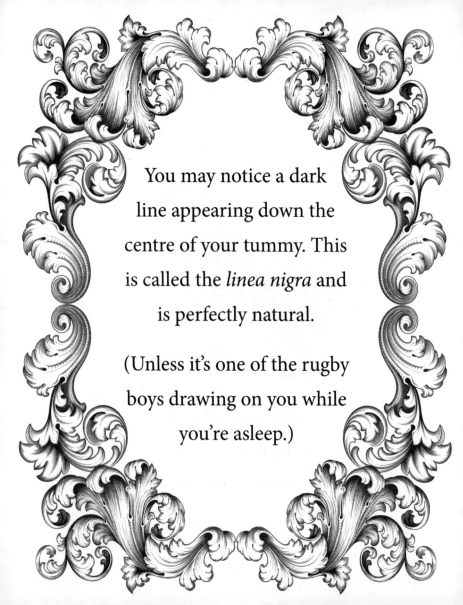

You may notice a dark line appearing down the centre of your tummy. This is called the *linea nigra* and is perfectly natural.

(Unless it's one of the rugby boys drawing on you while you're asleep.)

At 15 weeks your
baby is the size of a
small avocado.

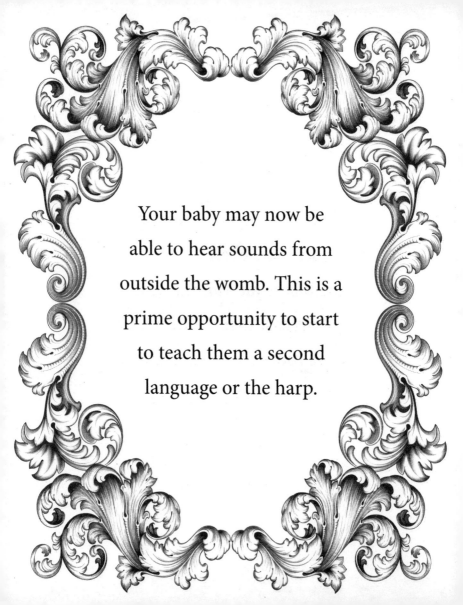

Your baby may now be able to hear sounds from outside the womb. This is a prime opportunity to start to teach them a second language or the harp.

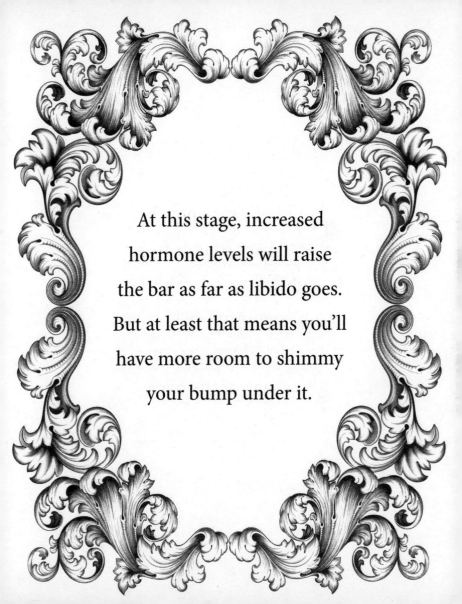

At this stage, increased hormone levels will raise the bar as far as libido goes. But at least that means you'll have more room to shimmy your bump under it.

Having sex while pregnant can sometimes be uncomfortable, so make sure you have the best mattress money can buy, good quality pillows and 1,000 thread-count sheets.

'Rear entry' (aka 'Corgi
style') is a good position
for pregnant women,
as is 'The Throne'.

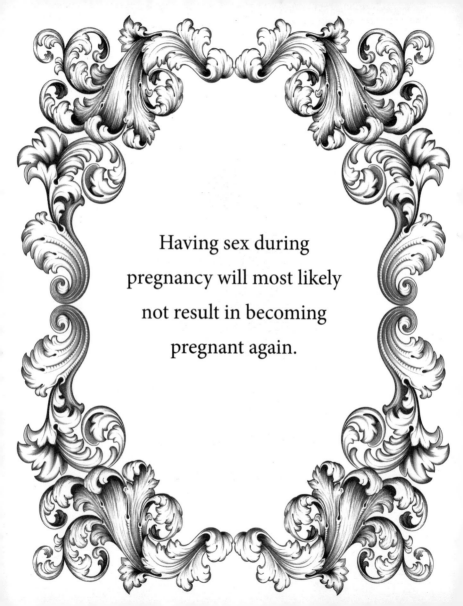

Having sex during pregnancy will most likely not result in becoming pregnant again.

At 16 weeks your
baby is the size of a
pomegranate.

For summer pregnancies sunglasses can be a stylish way of keeping bright light from your eyes.

For winter pregnancies a good way to keep warm in the cold weather is to wear winter clothing. Think jumpers, coats and hats.

At 17 weeks your
baby is the size of a
goose egg.

You will probably undergo
lots of tests at this point.
Don't worry, though, you
won't need to revise.

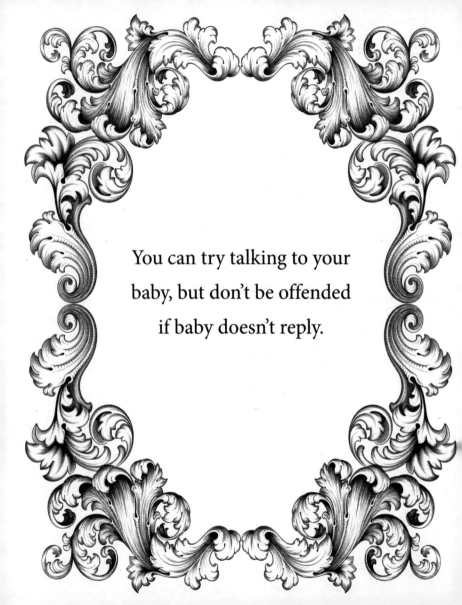

You can try talking to your
baby, but don't be offended
if baby doesn't reply.

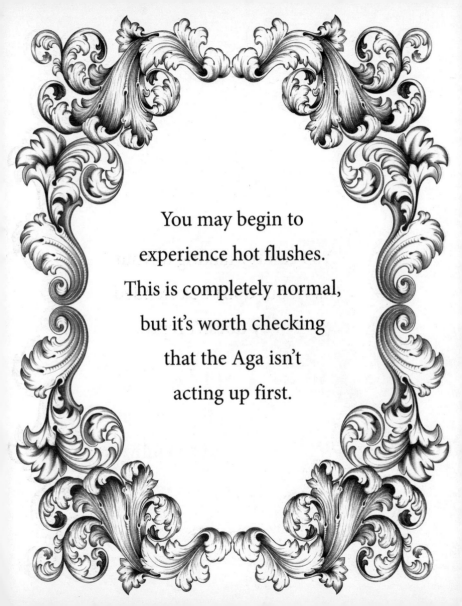

You may begin to experience hot flushes. This is completely normal, but it's worth checking that the Aga isn't acting up first.

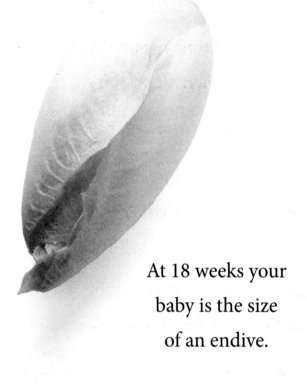

At 18 weeks your
baby is the size
of an endive.

*If you would like to know the sex of your baby, there are many advantages:*

❧ *Choosing a name that suits hereditary titles*

❧ *Briefing your interiors expert on nursery décor*

❧ *Finding the right personal shopper for baby's wardrobe*

❧ *Knowing whether to enrol your baby at Eton or Cheltenham Ladies' College*

❧ *Finding out if it's a boy or a girl*

❧ *You don't like surprises*

*If you do decide to choose your baby's name now, think carefully, as it will be the first impression your child makes.*

*In the olden days, names were taken from a list of special words (or 'names') like Tamarah, Dickon and Harry.*

*Nowadays literally any word can be a name, so the best rule of thumb is to try to choose something you'll be able to remember.*

**Good words for names:**

*Chard, Leylandii, Hellespont,*

*Aqua, Origami, Isotope, Inca,*

*Tikka, Nova*


**Bad words for names:**

*Guantanamo, Leland,*

*Chlamydia, Moist, Sepsis, Penge,*

*Vindaloo, Cortina, Fandabidozi*

*Double-barrelled names require*
*extra thought. Good examples include:*

*Henrietta Rogers-Thomas*

*Will Cooke-Bacon*

*Lottie Knockton-Wood*

*Tabitha Faulds-Coates*

*Binky Bowles-Balls*

*Alexander Irons-Curtain*

*Beatrice Brakes-Waters*

*Henry Banks-Wise-Lee*

*Hugh Luvsya-Baby*

At 19 weeks your
baby is the size
of a radicchio.

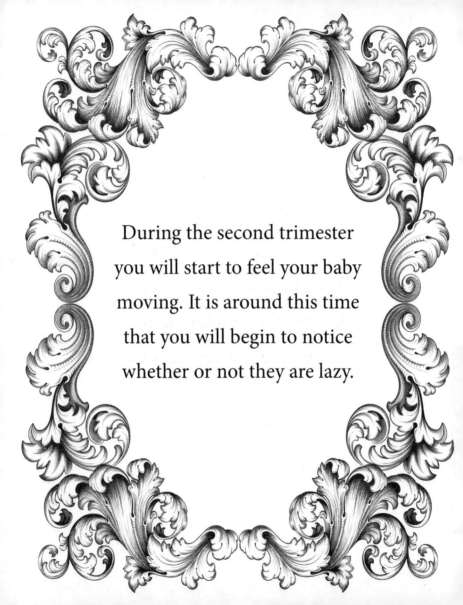

During the second trimester you will start to feel your baby moving. It is around this time that you will begin to notice whether or not they are lazy.

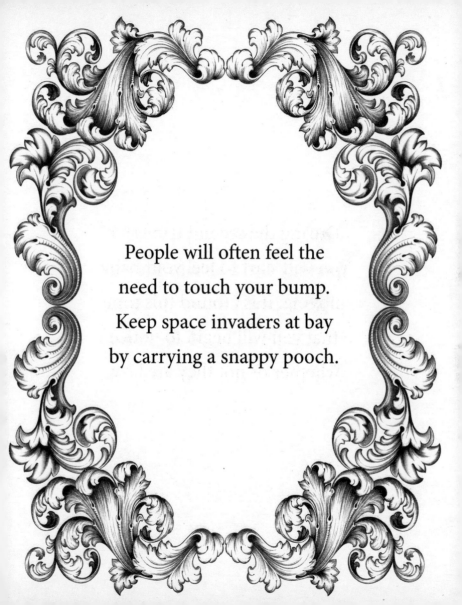

People will often feel the
need to touch your bump.
Keep space invaders at bay
by carrying a snappy pooch.

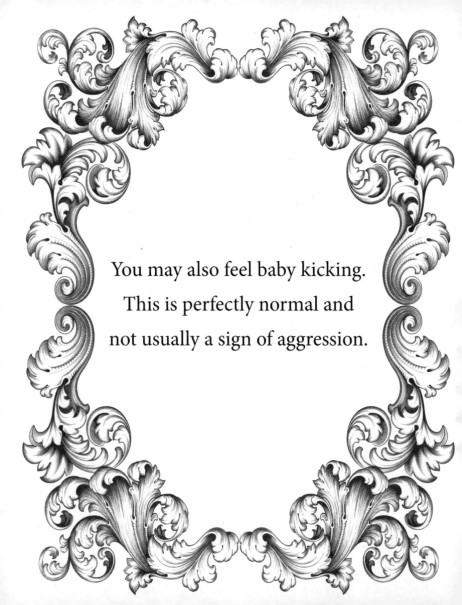

You may also feel baby kicking. This is perfectly normal and not usually a sign of aggression.

At 20 weeks your
baby is the size of a
Jerusalem artichoke.

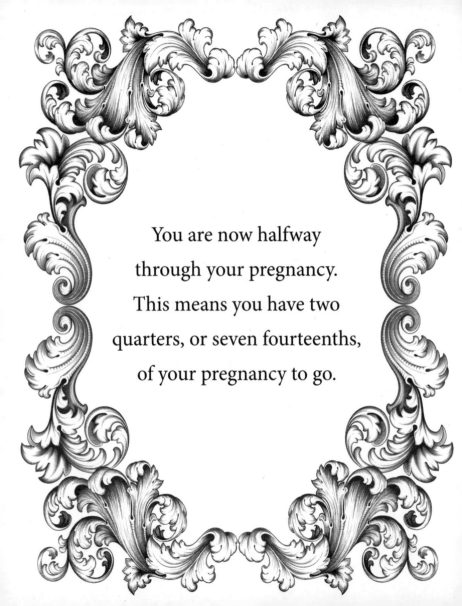

You are now halfway
through your pregnancy.
This means you have two
quarters, or seven fourteenths,
of your pregnancy to go.

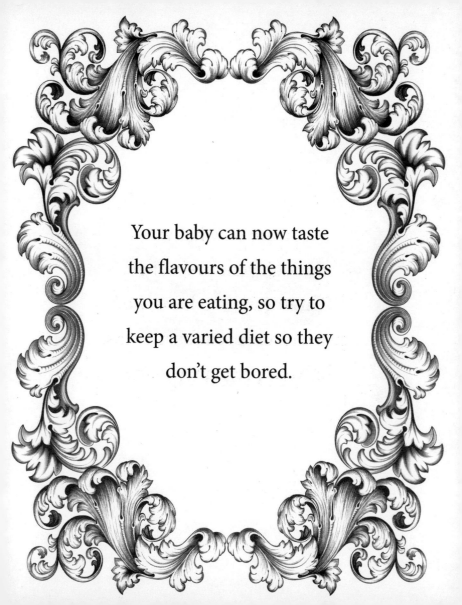

Your baby can now taste the flavours of the things you are eating, so try to keep a varied diet so they don't get bored.

At 21 weeks your
baby is as long as a
sweet potato.

You may occasionally
feel your baby hiccupping.
It is not appropriate to
shout 'Boo!' at it.

If your old clothes don't fit, why not buy new ones with extra space for your bump?

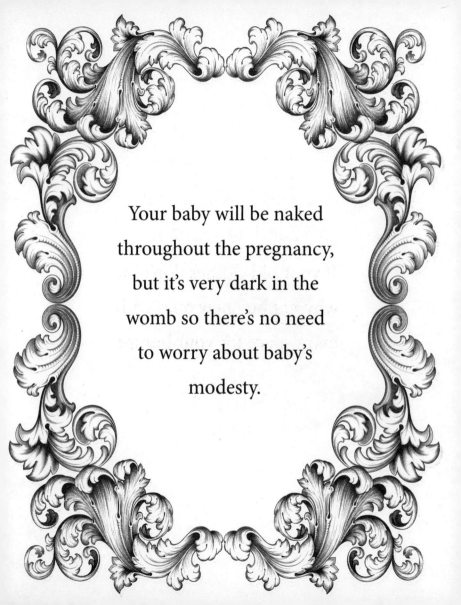

Your baby will be naked throughout the pregnancy, but it's very dark in the womb so there's no need to worry about baby's modesty.

At 22 weeks your
baby is as long as a
bunch of pak choi.

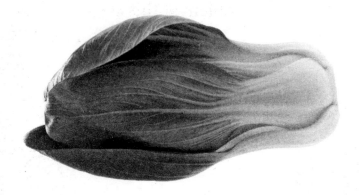

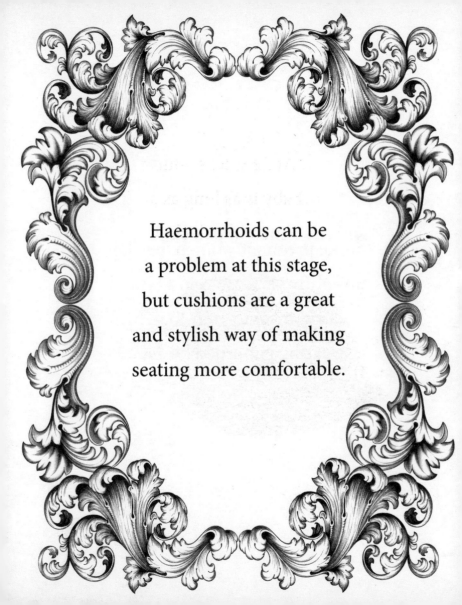

Haemorrhoids can be
a problem at this stage,
but cushions are a great
and stylish way of making
seating more comfortable.

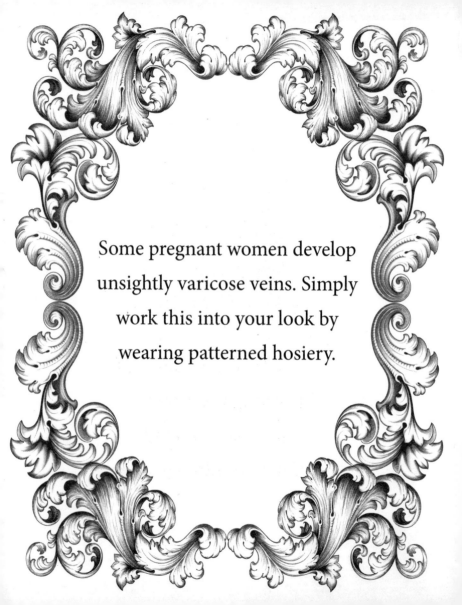

Some pregnant women develop unsightly varicose veins. Simply work this into your look by wearing patterned hosiery.

At 23 weeks your
baby weighs the same
as just over a pound
of muscovado sugar.

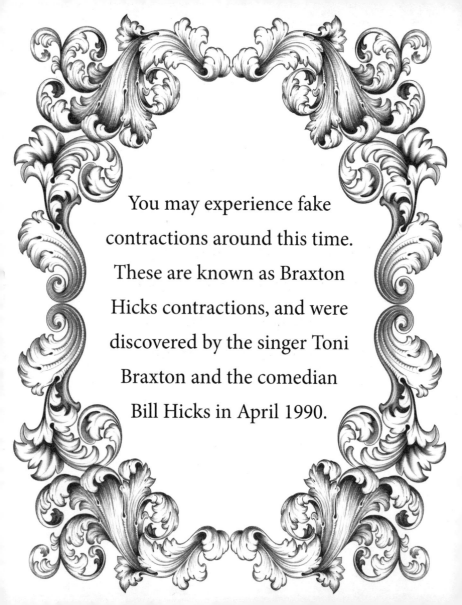

You may experience fake contractions around this time. These are known as Braxton Hicks contractions, and were discovered by the singer Toni Braxton and the comedian Bill Hicks in April 1990.

At 23 weeks baby can feel you dance, so set a good example by working on your pointe technique.

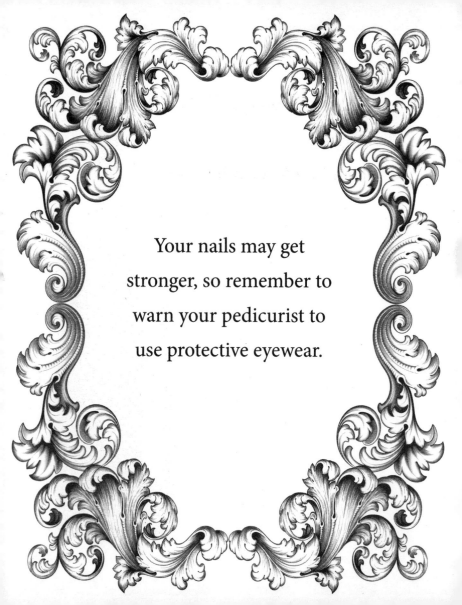

Your nails may get stronger, so remember to warn your pedicurist to use protective eyewear.

At 24 weeks your baby is
as long as a 750ml bottle of
Château Mouton Rothschild.

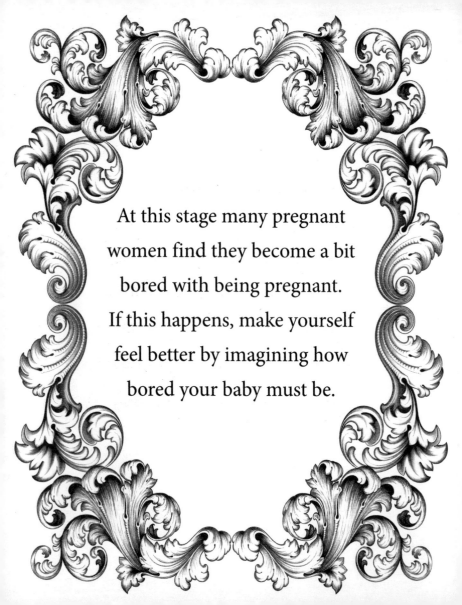

At this stage many pregnant women find they become a bit bored with being pregnant. If this happens, make yourself feel better by imagining how bored your baby must be.

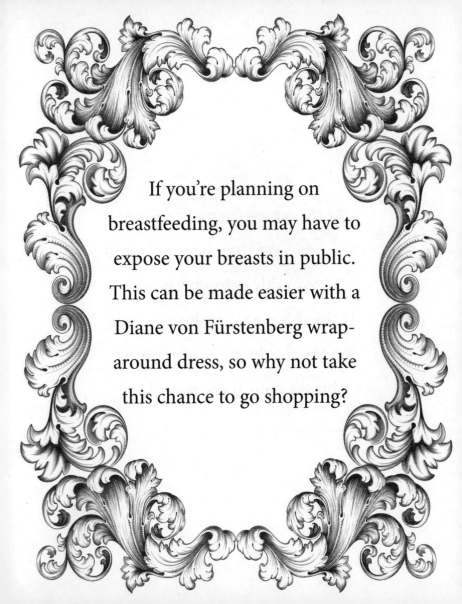

If you're planning on breastfeeding, you may have to expose your breasts in public. This can be made easier with a Diane von Fürstenberg wrap-around dress, so why not take this chance to go shopping?

At 25 weeks your
baby is the weight
of a celeriac.

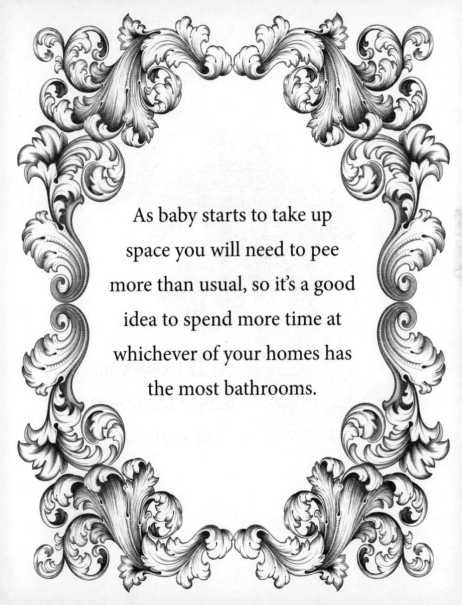

As baby starts to take up space you will need to pee more than usual, so it's a good idea to spend more time at whichever of your homes has the most bathrooms.

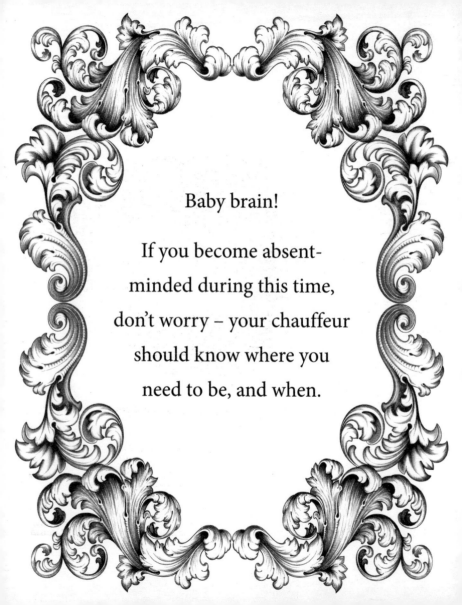

Baby brain!

If you become absent-
minded during this time,
don't worry – your chauffeur
should know where you
need to be, and when.

At 26 weeks your
baby is the length of
an English cucumber.

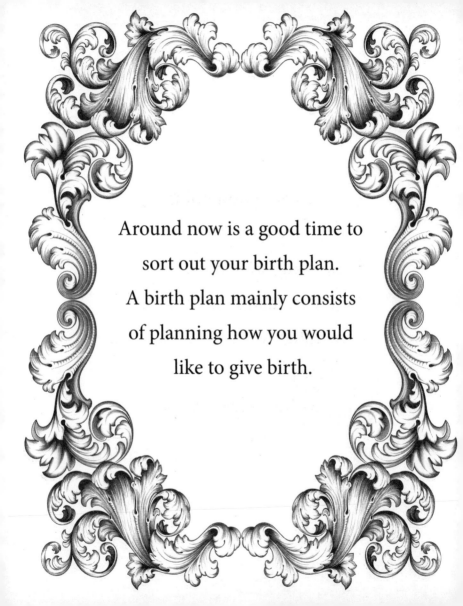

Around now is a good time to
sort out your birth plan.
A birth plan mainly consists
of planning how you would
like to give birth.

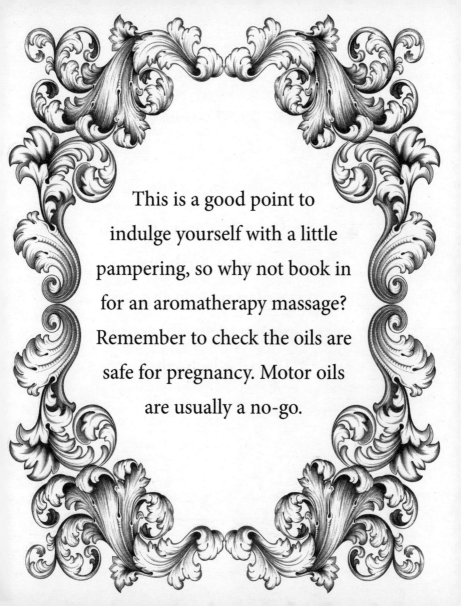

This is a good point to indulge yourself with a little pampering, so why not book in for an aromatherapy massage? Remember to check the oils are safe for pregnancy. Motor oils are usually a no-go.

At 27 weeks your baby is
as long as a Magnum of
Bollinger Special Cuvée.

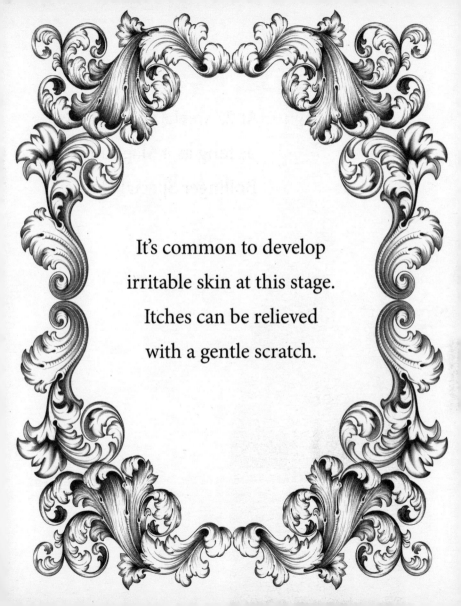

It's common to develop
irritable skin at this stage.
Itches can be relieved
with a gentle scratch.

Some mothers like to sing
to baby. Singing lessons
now can save on the cost
of counselling later.

At 28 weeks your
baby is the length of a
Chinese cabbage.

# The Third Trimester: Eminence Imminent

At 29 weeks your baby
weighs as much as an
ostrich egg.

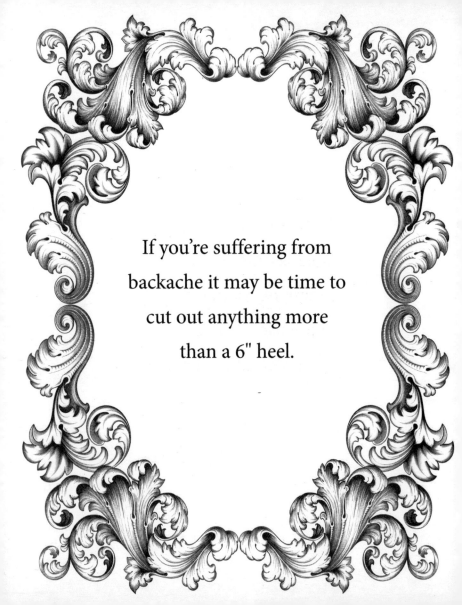

If you're suffering from backache it may be time to cut out anything more than a 6" heel.

If you suffer from embarrassing wind during pregnancy, a pooch can provide useful cover for any unpleasant smells.

At 30 weeks your baby weighs as much as a 3lb packet of squid ink pasta.

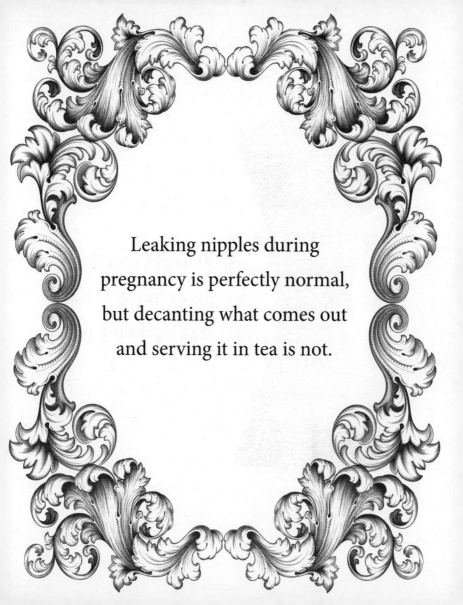

Leaking nipples during pregnancy is perfectly normal, but decanting what comes out and serving it in tea is not.

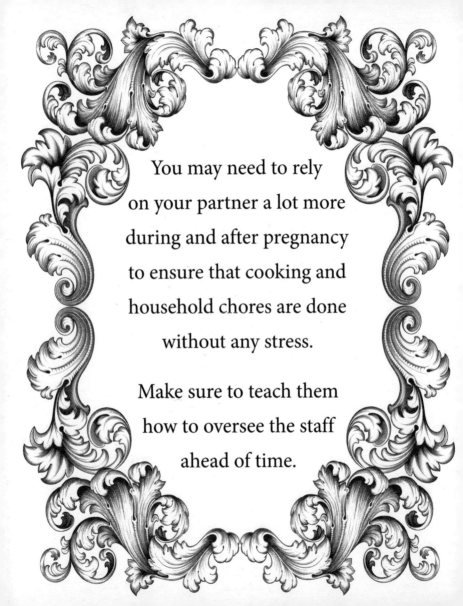

You may need to rely on your partner a lot more during and after pregnancy to ensure that cooking and household chores are done without any stress.

Make sure to teach them how to oversee the staff ahead of time.

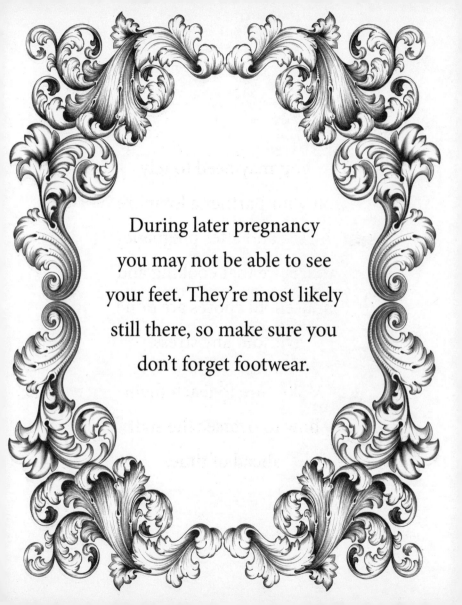

During later pregnancy you may not be able to see your feet. They're most likely still there, so make sure you don't forget footwear.

At 31 weeks your baby weighs
as much as 3 papayas.

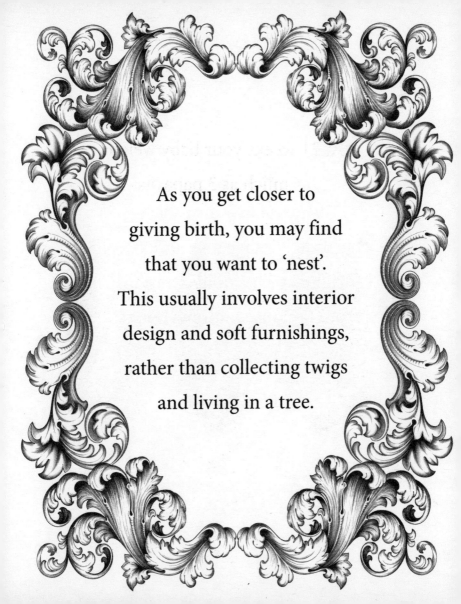

As you get closer to giving birth, you may find that you want to 'nest'. This usually involves interior design and soft furnishings, rather than collecting twigs and living in a tree.

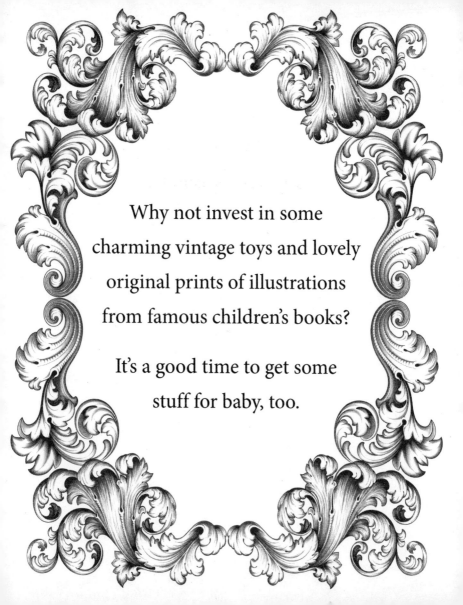

Why not invest in some charming vintage toys and lovely original prints of illustrations from famous children's books?

It's a good time to get some stuff for baby, too.

At 32 weeks your
baby weighs as much
as 7 fennel bulbs.

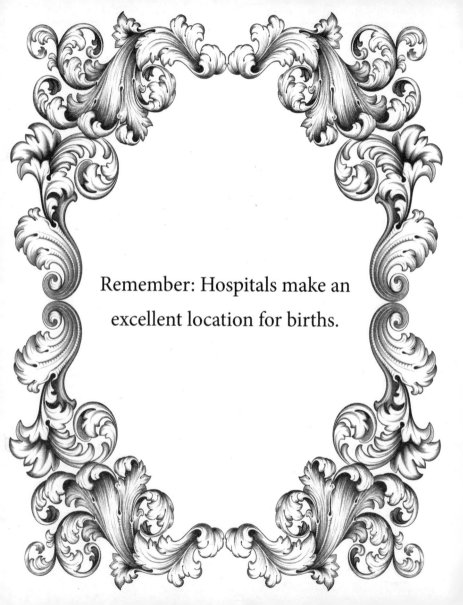

Remember: Hospitals make an excellent location for births.

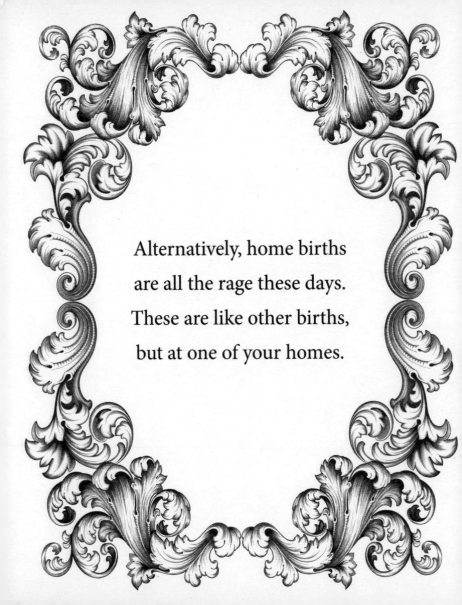

Alternatively, home births are all the rage these days. These are like other births, but at one of your homes.

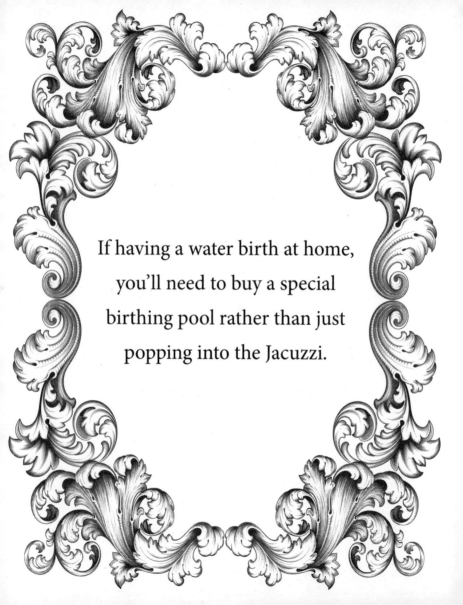

If having a water birth at home, you'll need to buy a special birthing pool rather than just popping into the Jacuzzi.

At 33 weeks your baby weighs as much
as just over 5lbs of langoustines.

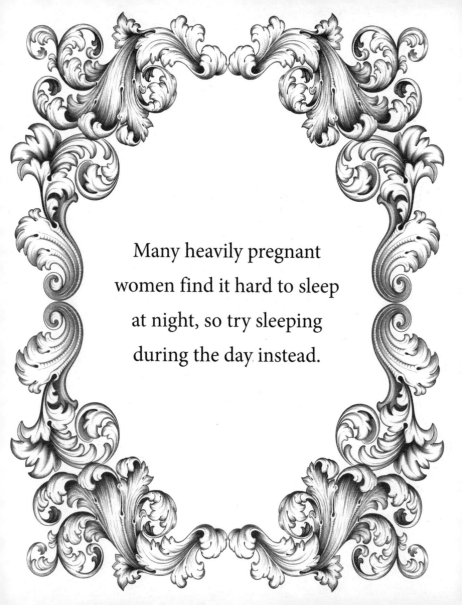

Many heavily pregnant
women find it hard to sleep
at night, so try sleeping
during the day instead.

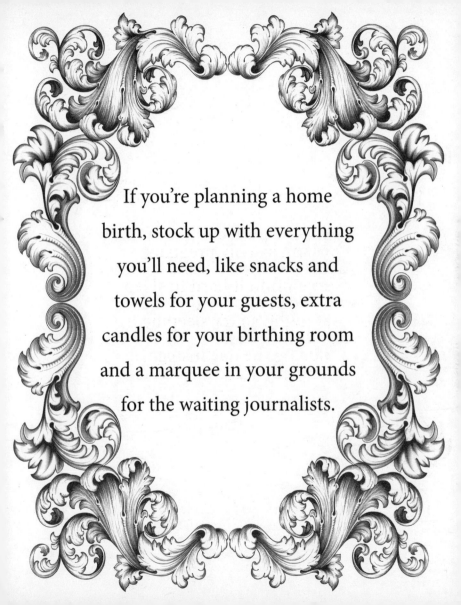

If you're planning a home birth, stock up with everything you'll need, like snacks and towels for your guests, extra candles for your birthing room and a marquee in your grounds for the waiting journalists.

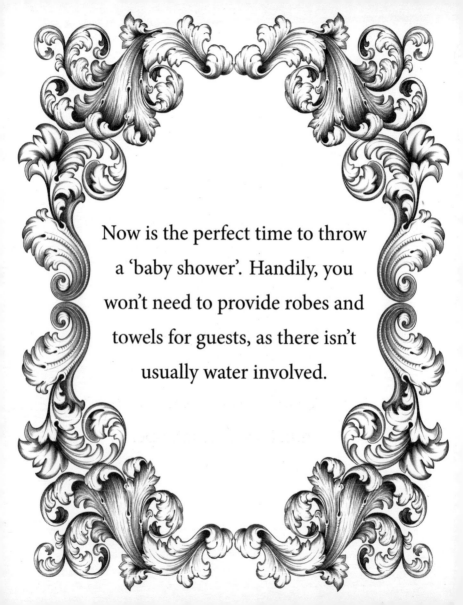

Now is the perfect time to throw a 'baby shower'. Handily, you won't need to provide robes and towels for guests, as there isn't usually water involved.

At 34 weeks your baby weighs

as much as a cantaloupe.

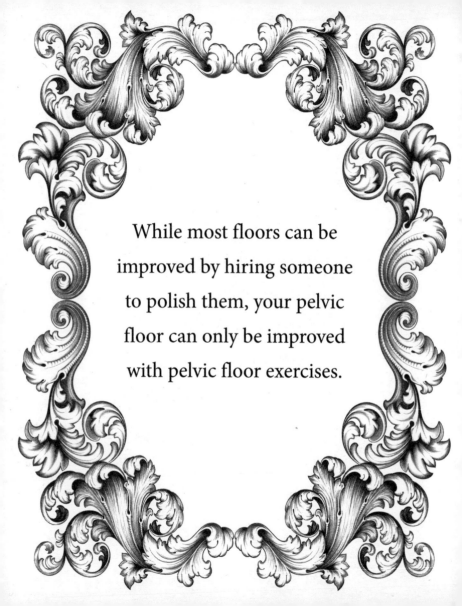

While most floors can be improved by hiring someone to polish them, your pelvic floor can only be improved with pelvic floor exercises.

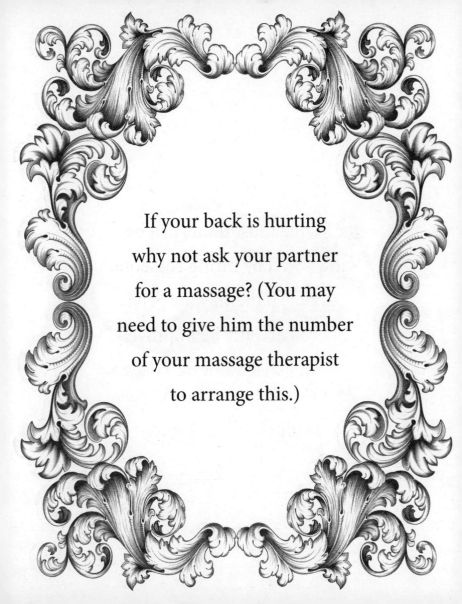

If your back is hurting
why not ask your partner
for a massage? (You may
need to give him the number
of your massage therapist
to arrange this.)

At 35 weeks your baby weighs

as much as a coconut.

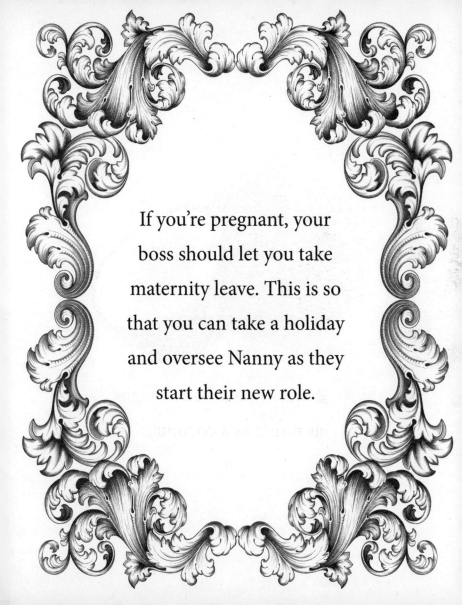

If you're pregnant, your boss should let you take maternity leave. This is so that you can take a holiday and oversee Nanny as they start their new role.

NCT weekends are popular last-minute antenatal classes, which I believe take place in multi-storey car parks.

At 36 weeks your baby
is as long as a haunch
of venison.

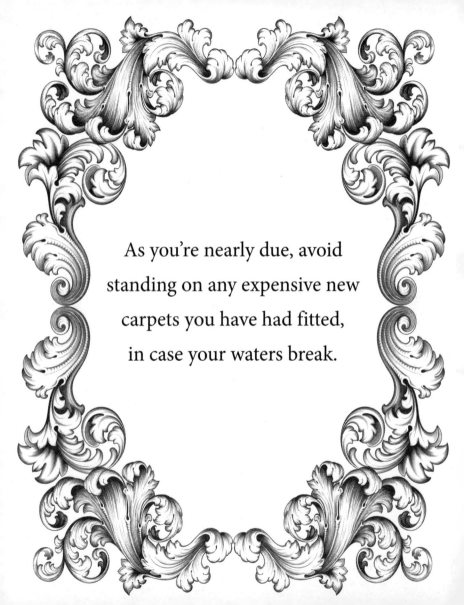

As you're nearly due, avoid
standing on any expensive new
carpets you have had fitted,
in case your waters break.

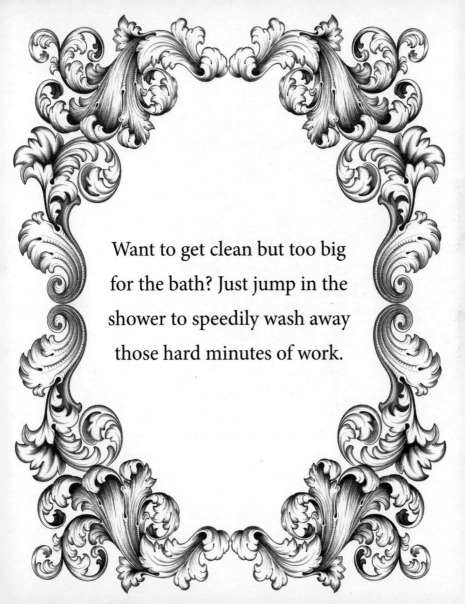

Want to get clean but too big for the bath? Just jump in the shower to speedily wash away those hard minutes of work.

At 37 weeks your baby is as long as a stalk of Swiss chard.

In order to bring baby home from the hospital you're going to need a car seat, so remind your driver to pick one up as the due date draws near.

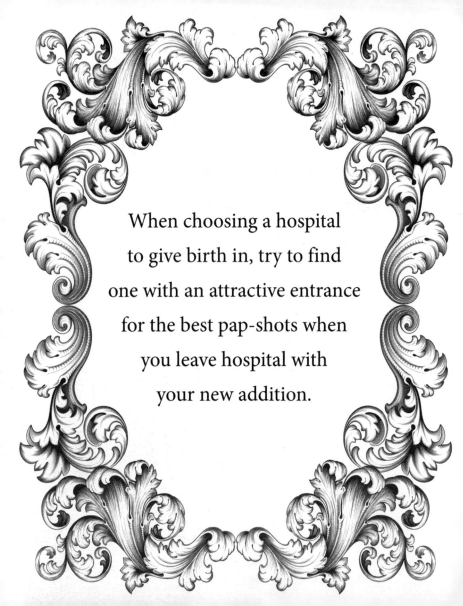

When choosing a hospital
to give birth in, try to find
one with an attractive entrance
for the best pap-shots when
you leave hospital with
your new addition.

At 38 weeks your baby is as long as a Jeroboam of Champagne.

*Don't forget to pack a bag of things you'll need at the hospital, including:*

- *Harper's Bazaar*

- *iPad*

- *Make-up bag*

- *Hairdryer*

- *Scatter cushions*

- *Massage oil*

- *Crème de la Mer*

- *Elizabeth Arden Eight Hour Cream*

- *Wardrobe changes for photographs*

- *HD digi-cam (if you haven't hired a professional crew)*

*The doctors and nurses will provide most of the medical bits, so don't worry too much about those.*

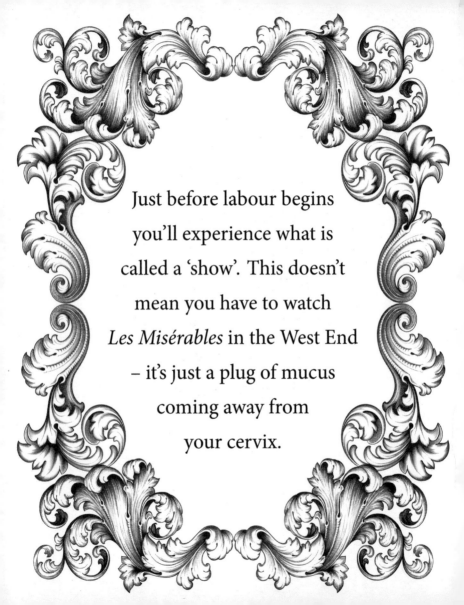

Just before labour begins you'll experience what is called a 'show'. This doesn't mean you have to watch *Les Misérables* in the West End – it's just a plug of mucus coming away from your cervix.

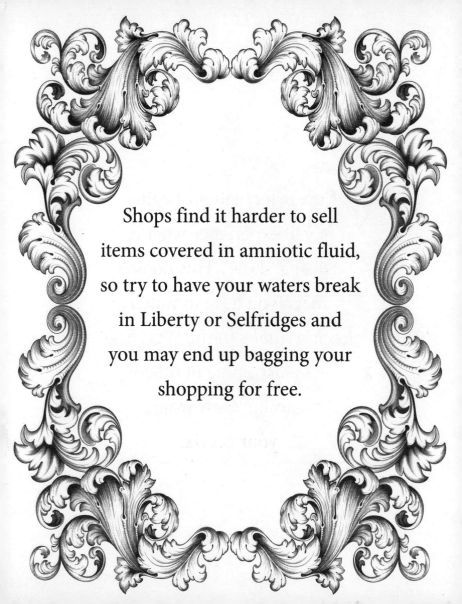

Shops find it harder to sell items covered in amniotic fluid, so try to have your waters break in Liberty or Selfridges and you may end up bagging your shopping for free.

At 39 weeks
your baby is as
long as a head
of kale.

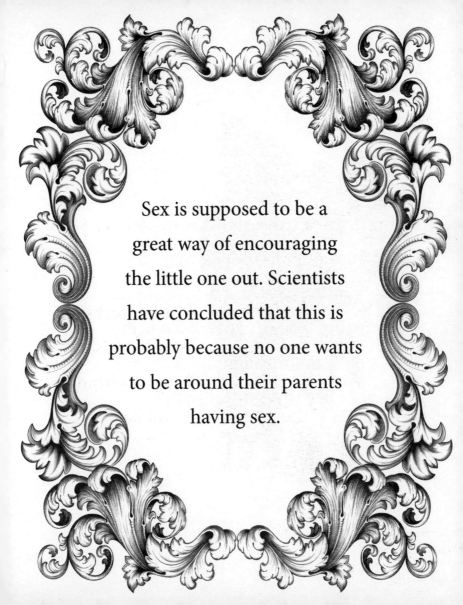

Sex is supposed to be a great way of encouraging the little one out. Scientists have concluded that this is probably because no one wants to be around their parents having sex.

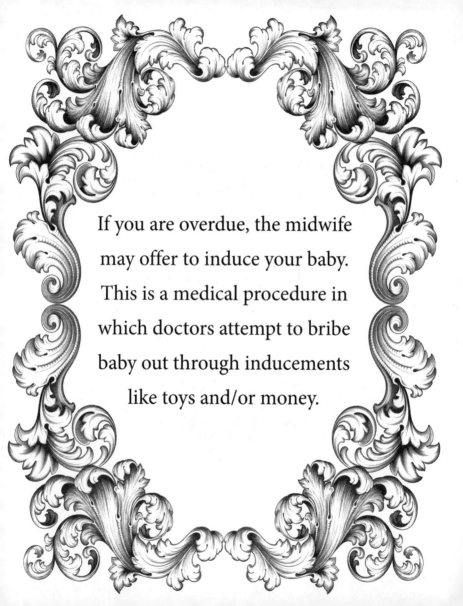

If you are overdue, the midwife may offer to induce your baby. This is a medical procedure in which doctors attempt to bribe baby out through inducements like toys and/or money.

# Labour

*Now that your bags are packed and your driver is on alert, you're ready to go into labour (you might prefer the Conservatives or the Liberal Democrats, but I wouldn't spend too much time canvassing as you're about to have a baby).*

*Despite your baby growing from an egg, they won't hatch by themselves – you will have to give birth to them.*

*There are lots of different ways to give birth but the main thing to focus on is that the baby needs to leave your womb.*

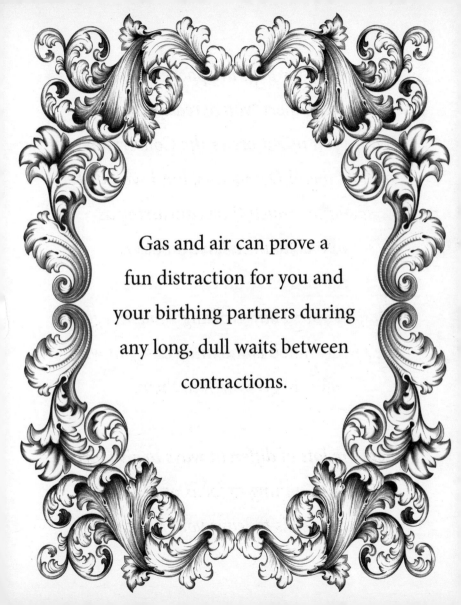

Gas and air can prove a
fun distraction for you and
your birthing partners during
any long, dull waits between
contractions.

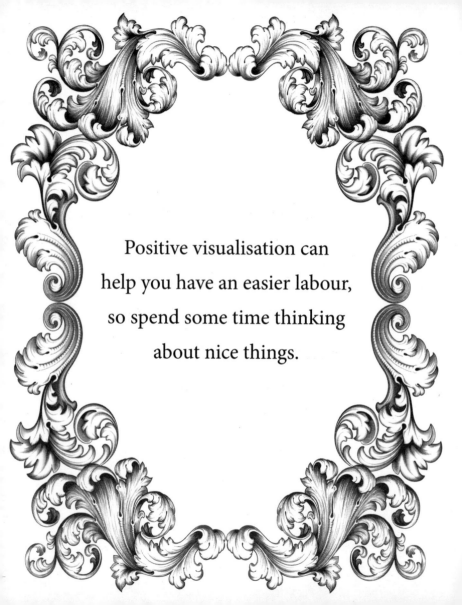

Positive visualisation can
help you have an easier labour,
so spend some time thinking
about nice things.

A breech birth is when your baby comes out bottom-first. It's often harder than a head-first birth, probably because baby can't see where he or she is going.

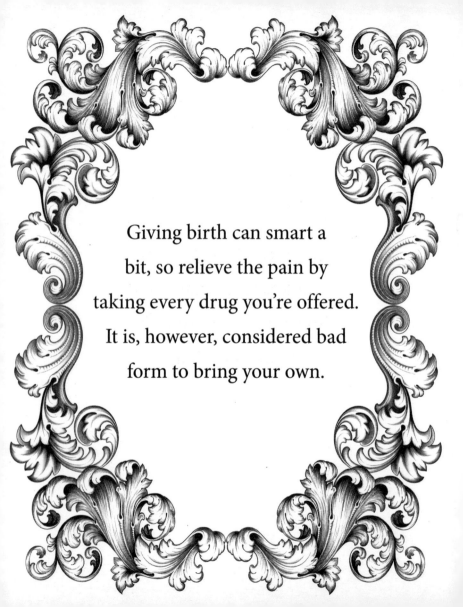

Giving birth can smart a
bit, so relieve the pain by
taking every drug you're offered.
It is, however, considered bad
form to bring your own.

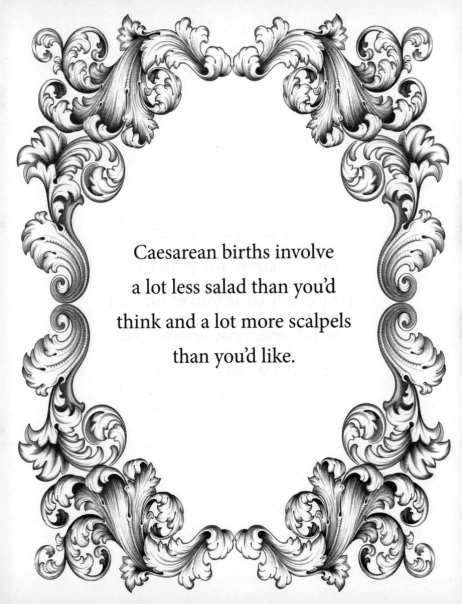

Caesarean births involve
a lot less salad than you'd
think and a lot more scalpels
than you'd like.

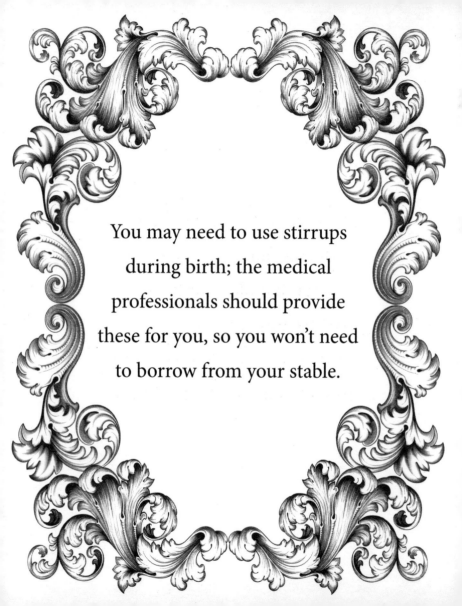

You may need to use stirrups during birth; the medical professionals should provide these for you, so you won't need to borrow from your stable.

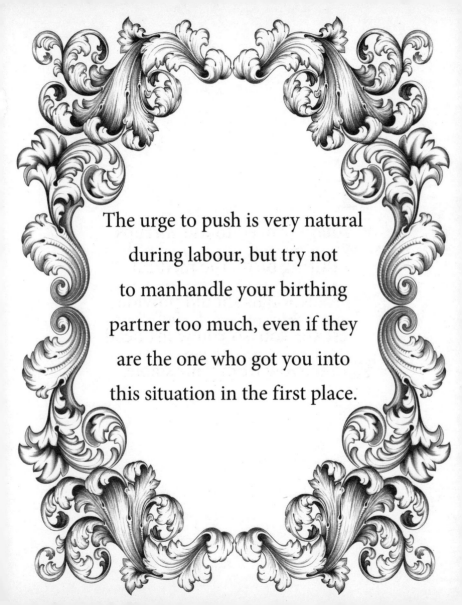

The urge to push is very natural during labour, but try not to manhandle your birthing partner too much, even if they are the one who got you into this situation in the first place.

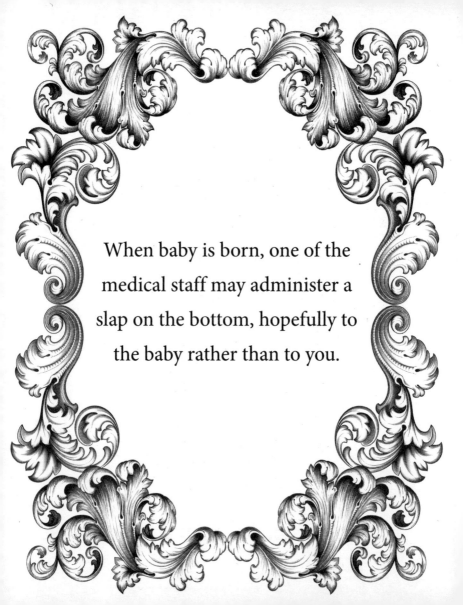

When baby is born, one of the
medical staff may administer a
slap on the bottom, hopefully to
the baby rather than to you.

At 40 weeks your baby
is the size and shape of
a newborn baby.

# After Birth:
# The First Year

*Once you've given birth, this means*
*that you are no longer pregnant*
*and are now a parent.*

*Being a parent means you*
*have a child, so remember to take*
*it home from the hospital.*

*If you are a lady, you will be*
*the infant's mother.*

*If you are a gentleman,*
*this usually means that you*
*are the little one's father.*

*Parenting can be quite daunting, but remember, you are not alone – you'll have your partner and family, nanny, housekeeper, nutritionist, Pilates instructor and psychic who can help you adjust to this exciting new period of your life.*

*In the first month or so you will spend a lot of time feeding and changing your baby, so it's unlikely you will be able to attend your usual social engagements. But don't feel down, as there is no reason that your friends at* Hello! *can't come to you instead.*

If you haven't done so already, don't forget to name your baby, as you'll need something to call it.

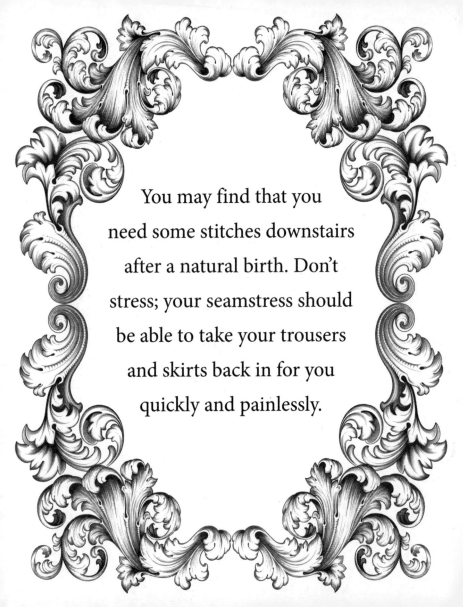

You may find that you need some stitches downstairs after a natural birth. Don't stress; your seamstress should be able to take your trousers and skirts back in for you quickly and painlessly.

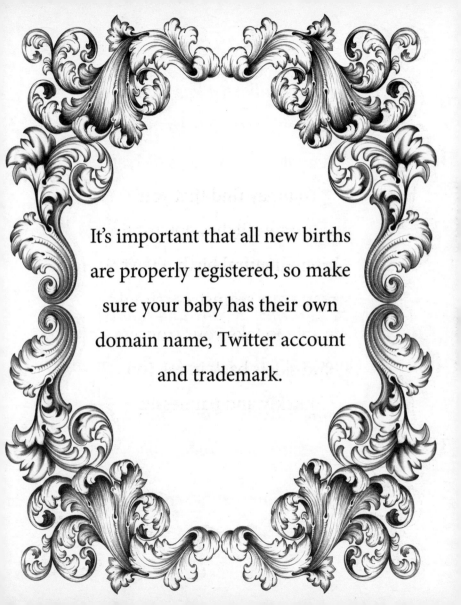

It's important that all new births are properly registered, so make sure your baby has their own domain name, Twitter account and trademark.

*Your baby will need lots of attention when they are so tiny, so make sure you follow these steps to keep your baby safe and well:*

❧ *Don't put baby near a naked flame*

❧ *Don't leave baby unattended*

❧ *Don't give baby any sharp instruments*

❧ *Don't leave baby on a high surface such as a window sill*

❧ *Don't let baby get too cold or too hot*

- *Don't give baby any firearms*

- *Don't let baby operate heavy machinery*

- *Don't put baby in a fridge or a freezer*

- *Don't put baby in the corner*

# 1–3 Months

At 1 month old, your
baby weighs as much
as a Pomeranian.

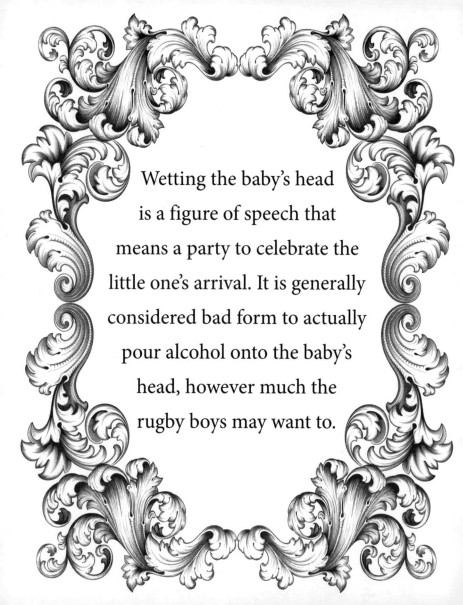

Wetting the baby's head is a figure of speech that means a party to celebrate the little one's arrival. It is generally considered bad form to actually pour alcohol onto the baby's head, however much the rugby boys may want to.

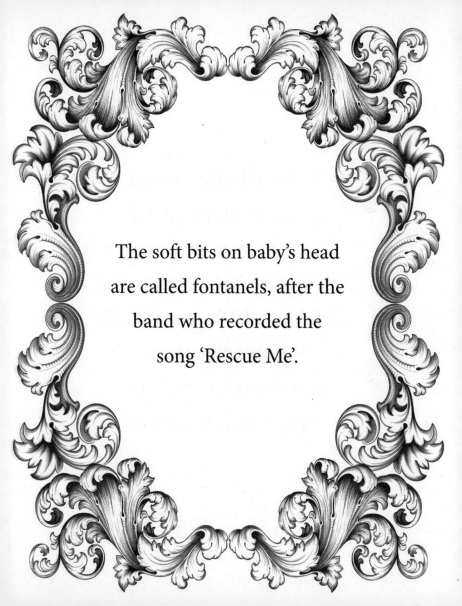

The soft bits on baby's head
are called fontanels, after the
band who recorded the
song 'Rescue Me'.

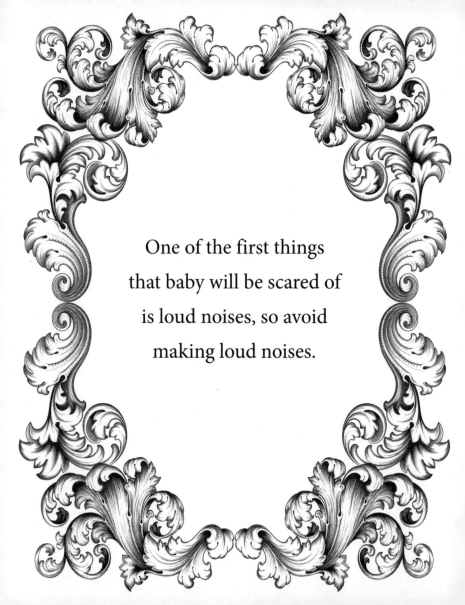

One of the first things
that baby will be scared of
is loud noises, so avoid
making loud noises.

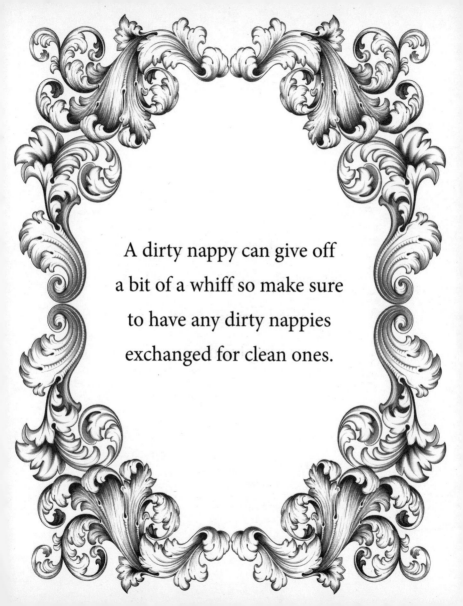

A dirty nappy can give off
a bit of a whiff so make sure
to have any dirty nappies
exchanged for clean ones.

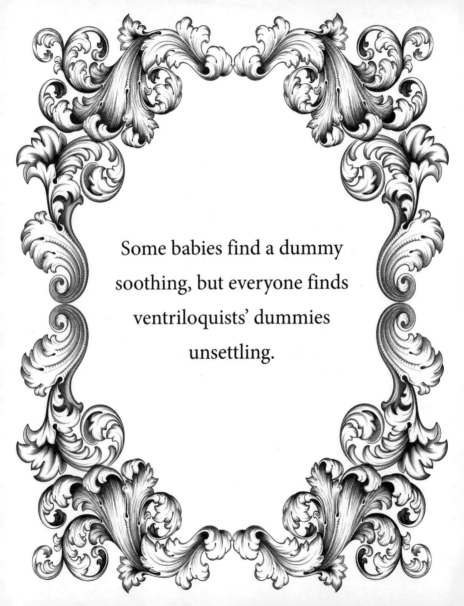

Some babies find a dummy soothing, but everyone finds ventriloquists' dummies unsettling.

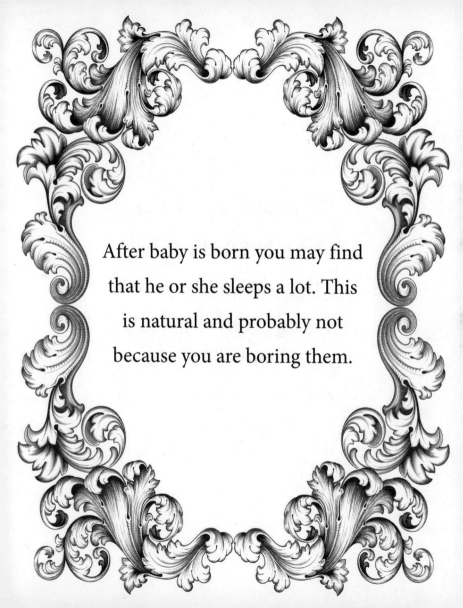

After baby is born you may find that he or she sleeps a lot. This is natural and probably not because you are boring them.

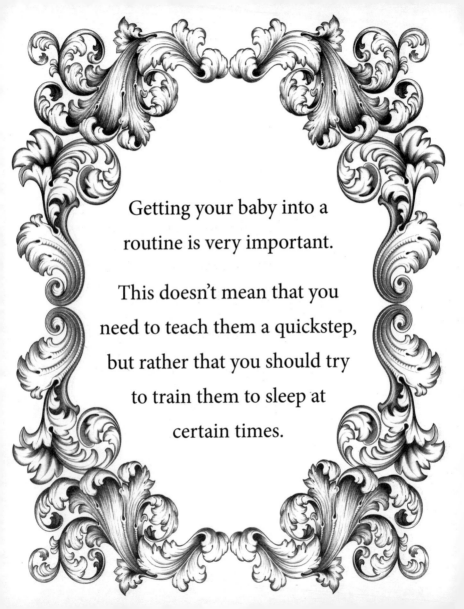

Getting your baby into a
routine is very important.

This doesn't mean that you
need to teach them a quickstep,
but rather that you should try
to train them to sleep at
certain times.

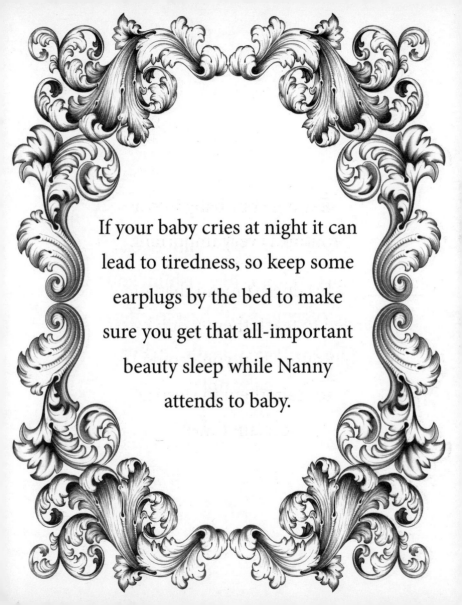

If your baby cries at night it can lead to tiredness, so keep some earplugs by the bed to make sure you get that all-important beauty sleep while Nanny attends to baby.

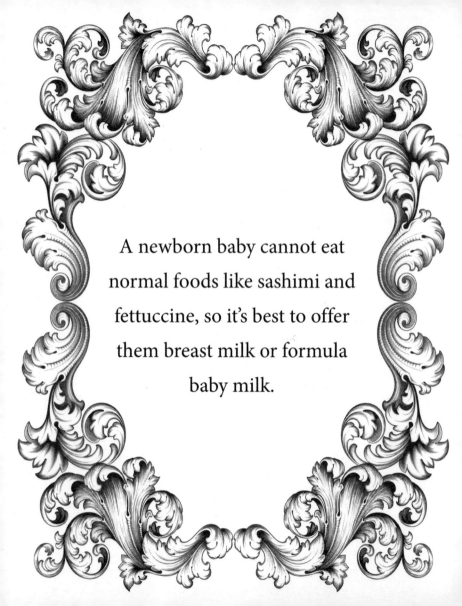

A newborn baby cannot eat normal foods like sashimi and fettuccine, so it's best to offer them breast milk or formula baby milk.

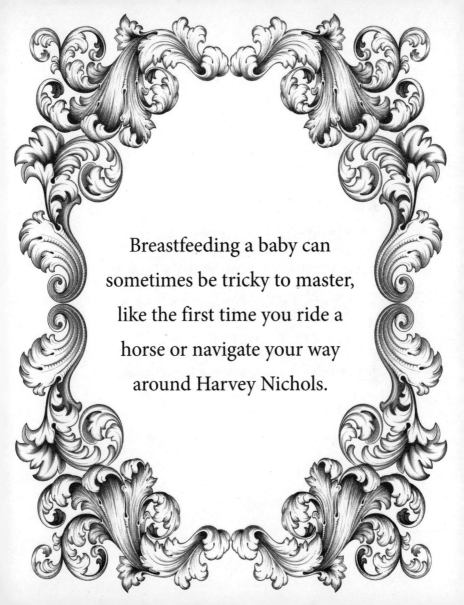

Breastfeeding a baby can sometimes be tricky to master, like the first time you ride a horse or navigate your way around Harvey Nichols.

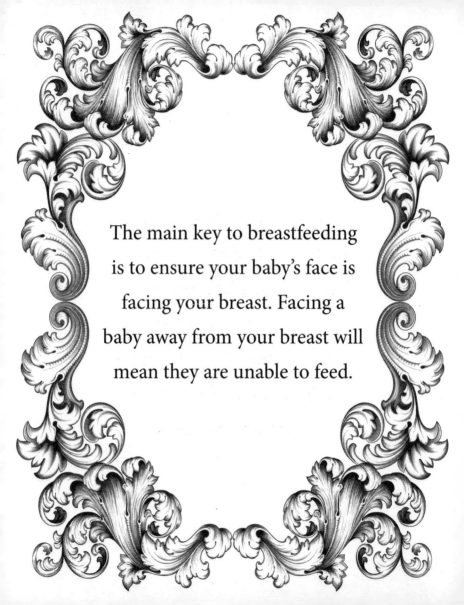

The main key to breastfeeding is to ensure your baby's face is facing your breast. Facing a baby away from your breast will mean they are unable to feed.

If you're breastfeeding you may need to express milk to feed baby at a later point. For this, buy a special breast milk pump rather than trying to adjust one you've picked up at Halfords.

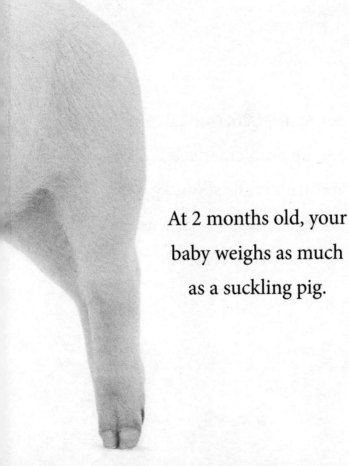

At 2 months old, your baby weighs as much as a suckling pig.

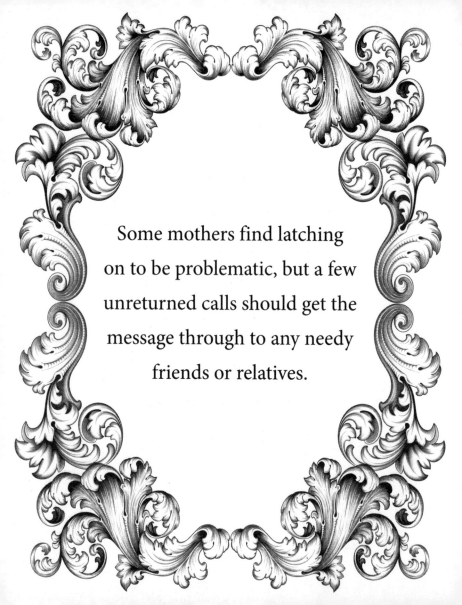

Some mothers find latching on to be problematic, but a few unreturned calls should get the message through to any needy friends or relatives.

A big decision you will need to make is whether you will go to your baby when they cry in the night, or let them cry themselves out.

This will mainly be decided by which wing of the house the baby's room is in.

Even from birth, baby will
be soothed by your voice,
so get Nanny to pop you on
speakerphone when you
call to check in.

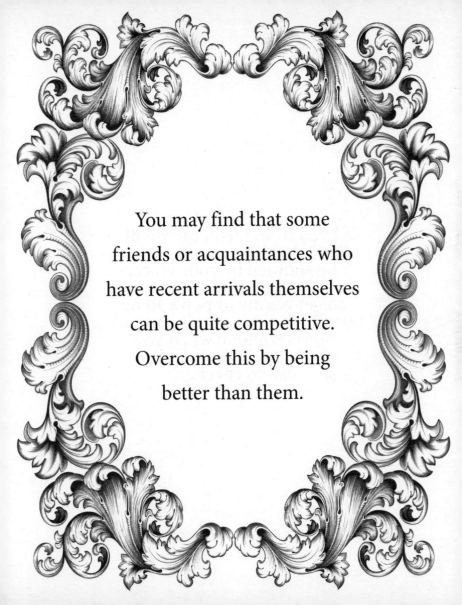

You may find that some friends or acquaintances who have recent arrivals themselves can be quite competitive. Overcome this by being better than them.

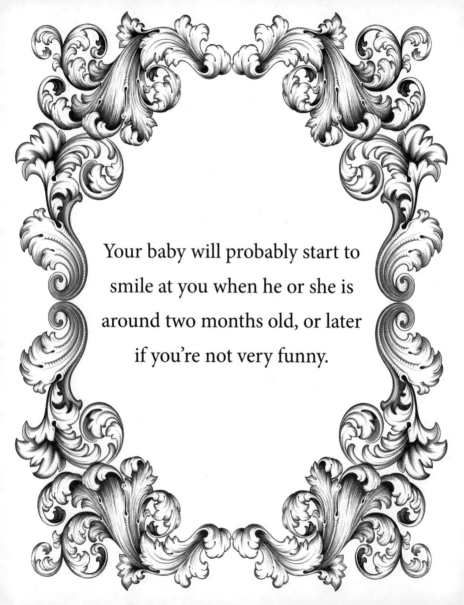

Your baby will probably start to smile at you when he or she is around two months old, or later if you're not very funny.

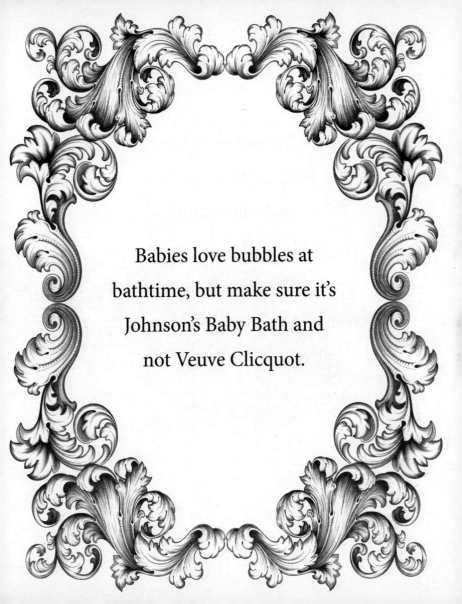

Babies love bubbles at bathtime, but make sure it's Johnson's Baby Bath and not Veuve Clicquot.

At 3 months old, your
baby is the length of a
small Masu salmon.

By this point, baby should be sleeping through the night and Nanny should begin to look much less tired.

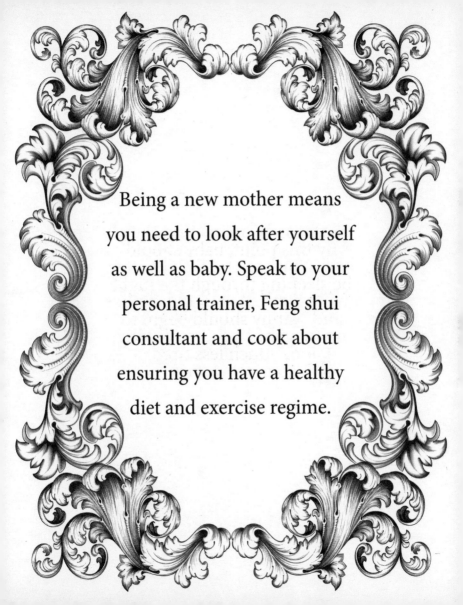

Being a new mother means you need to look after yourself as well as baby. Speak to your personal trainer, Feng shui consultant and cook about ensuring you have a healthy diet and exercise regime.

Some new mums find they have a bit of extra weight after giving birth. If your old clothes no longer fit you, try buying some new ones.

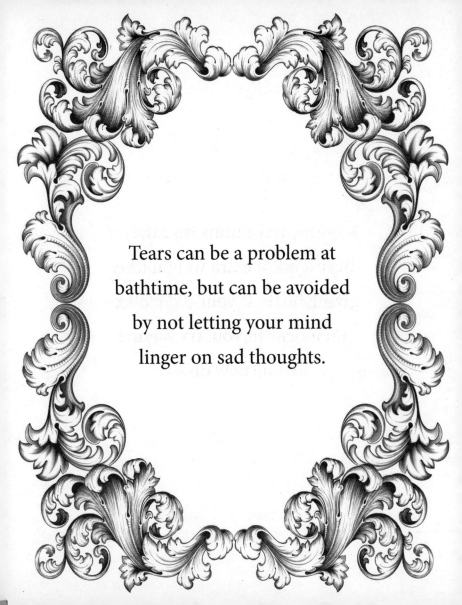

Tears can be a problem at bathtime, but can be avoided by not letting your mind linger on sad thoughts.

Baby massage is all the rage for helping baby relax and building the bond between mum and baby. Check yourselves into a spa for a bit of pampering.

When you take baby out you'll often need to use the 'baby changing room'. This is just for changing nappies, not for exchanging little ones you are disappointed with.

# 4–6 Months

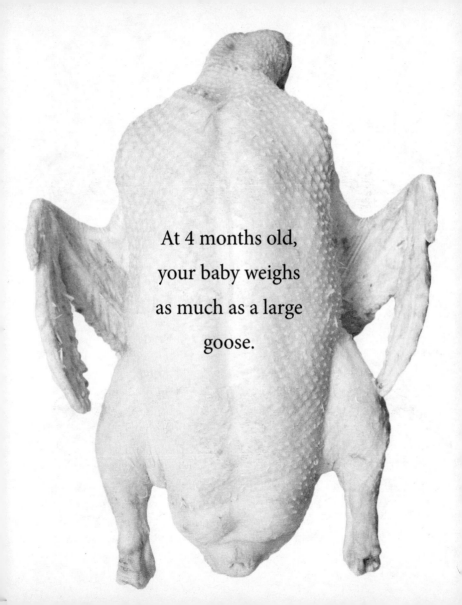

At 4 months old, your baby weighs as much as a large goose.

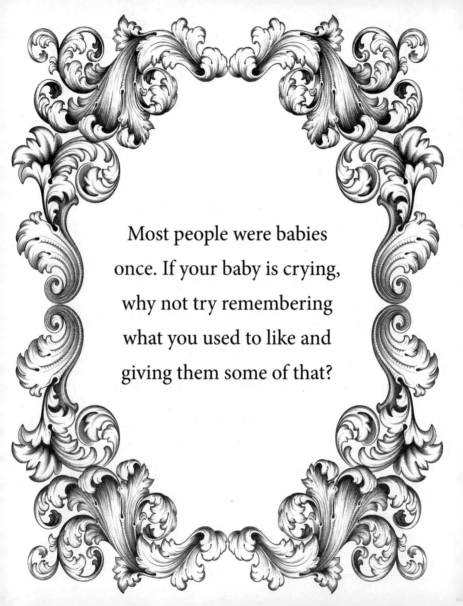

Most people were babies once. If your baby is crying, why not try remembering what you used to like and giving them some of that?

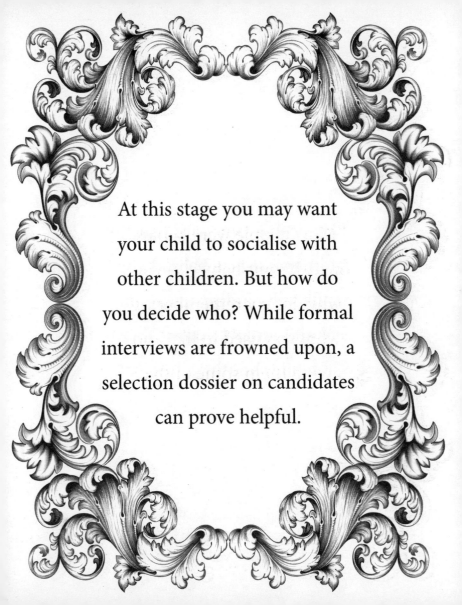

At this stage you may want your child to socialise with other children. But how do you decide who? While formal interviews are frowned upon, a selection dossier on candidates can prove helpful.

Play peek-a-boo with baby by hiding your face behind your hands or by hiding under their cot and jumping out at them while shouting, 'Boo!'

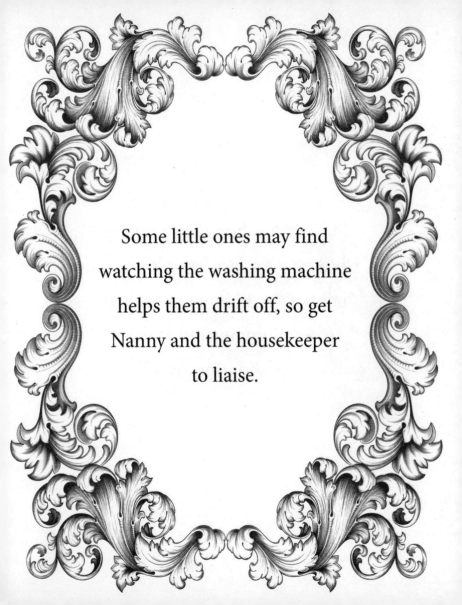

Some little ones may find
watching the washing machine
helps them drift off, so get
Nanny and the housekeeper
to liaise.

At 5 months old, your baby weighs as much as a Cavalier King Charles Spaniel.

*Babies grow very quickly. This means you will need to buy them clothes more regularly than just from the latest Spring/Summer or Autumn/Winter collections.*

*Don't stress, though; putting together a capsule wardrobe for your baby is one of the greatest joys of being a new mother.*

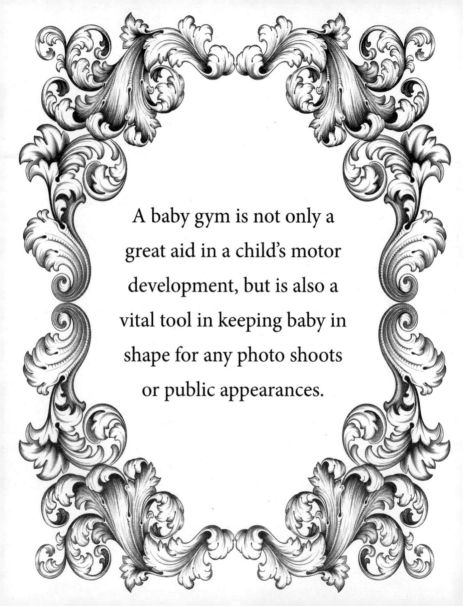

A baby gym is not only a great aid in a child's motor development, but is also a vital tool in keeping baby in shape for any photo shoots or public appearances.

Babies sometimes

wear babygros.

These are like tiny onesies.

At 6 months old, your baby
is the length of a lobster.

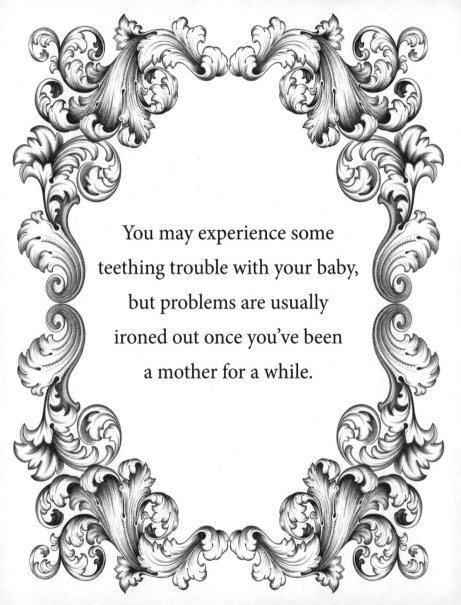

You may experience some
teething trouble with your baby,
but problems are usually
ironed out once you've been
a mother for a while.

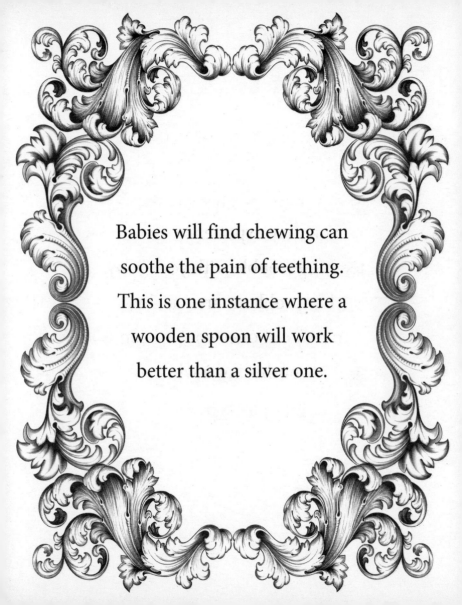

Babies will find chewing can soothe the pain of teething. This is one instance where a wooden spoon will work better than a silver one.

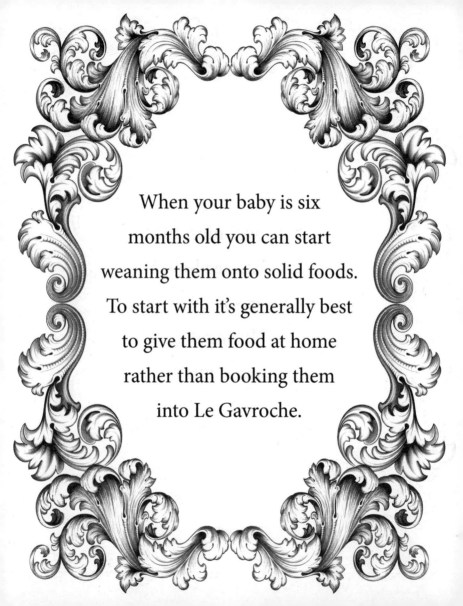

When your baby is six months old you can start weaning them onto solid foods. To start with it's generally best to give them food at home rather than booking them into Le Gavroche.

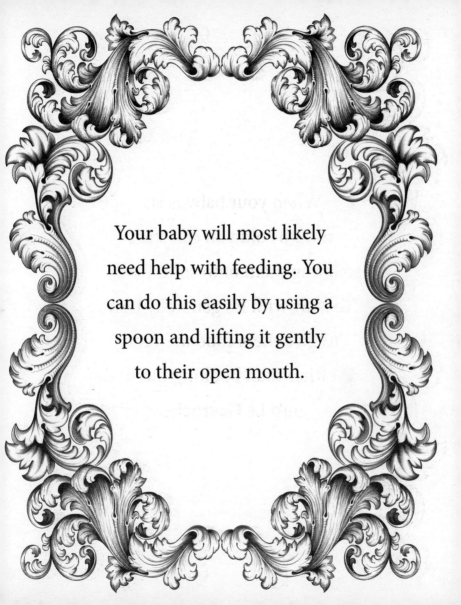

Your baby will most likely need help with feeding. You can do this easily by using a spoon and lifting it gently to their open mouth.

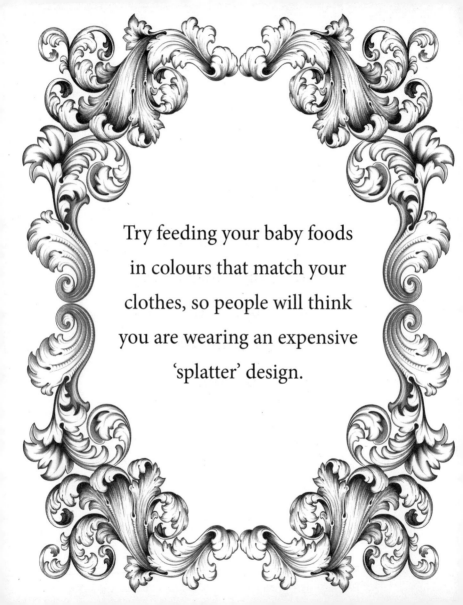

Try feeding your baby foods
in colours that match your
clothes, so people will think
you are wearing an expensive
'splatter' design.

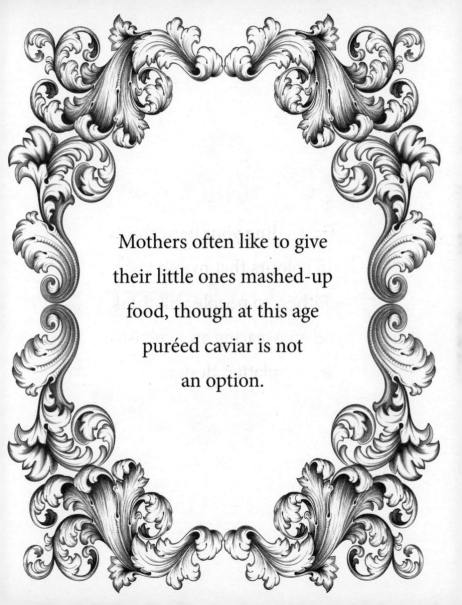

Mothers often like to give
their little ones mashed-up
food, though at this age
puréed caviar is not
an option.

# 7–12 Months

At 7 months old, your baby weighs
as much as 25 white truffles.

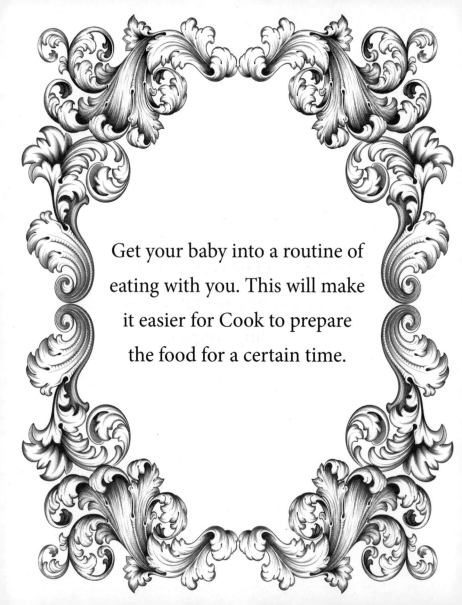

Get your baby into a routine of eating with you. This will make it easier for Cook to prepare the food for a certain time.

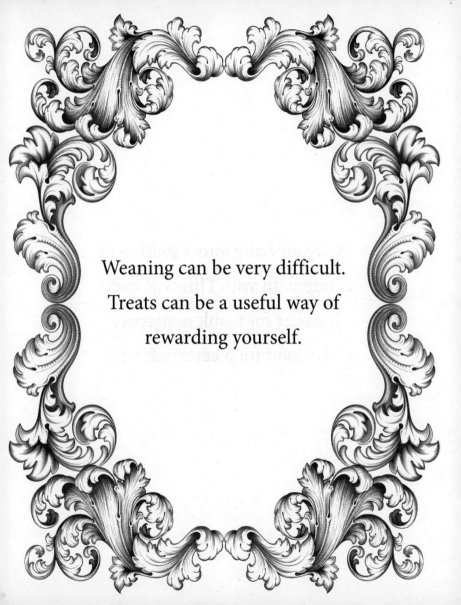

Weaning can be very difficult.
Treats can be a useful way of
rewarding yourself.

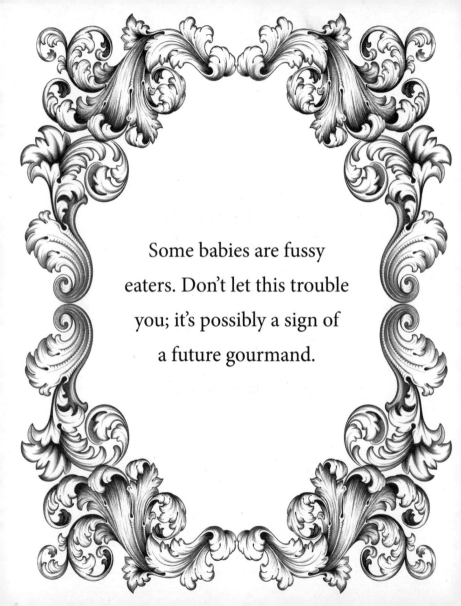

Some babies are fussy eaters. Don't let this trouble you; it's possibly a sign of a future gourmand.

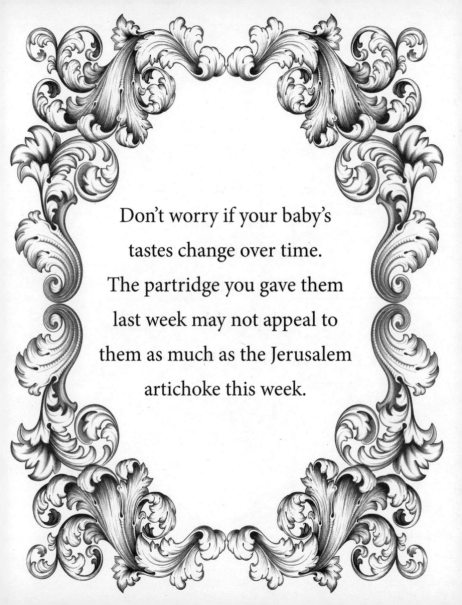

Don't worry if your baby's tastes change over time. The partridge you gave them last week may not appeal to them as much as the Jerusalem artichoke this week.

At 8 months old, your
baby is the length of a
dachshund.

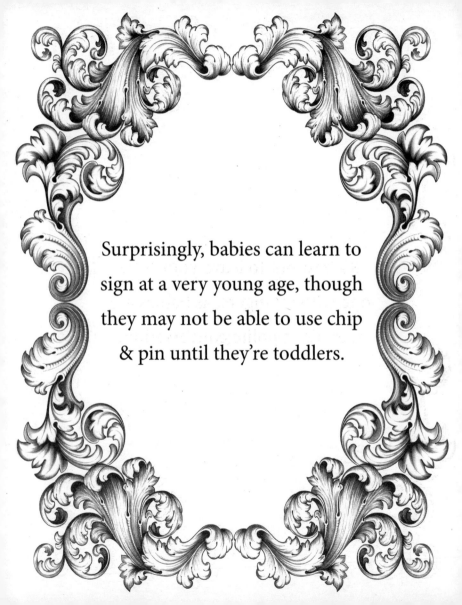

Surprisingly, babies can learn to sign at a very young age, though they may not be able to use chip & pin until they're toddlers.

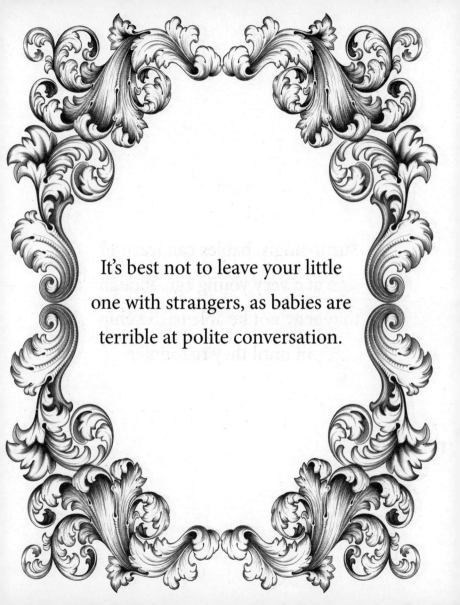

It's best not to leave your little one with strangers, as babies are terrible at polite conversation.

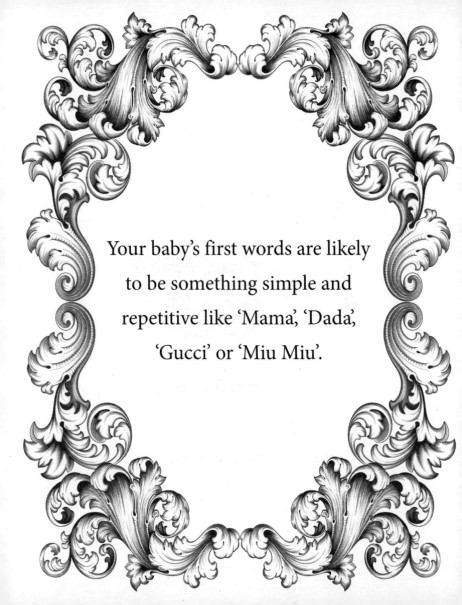

Your baby's first words are likely to be something simple and repetitive like 'Mama', 'Dada', 'Gucci' or 'Miu Miu'.

At 9 months old, your
baby weighs as much as
98 un-shucked oysters.

By around 9 months babies find that banging objects together is fun. Most develop beyond this, but some unfortunates become stuck at this stage and end up in rock bands.

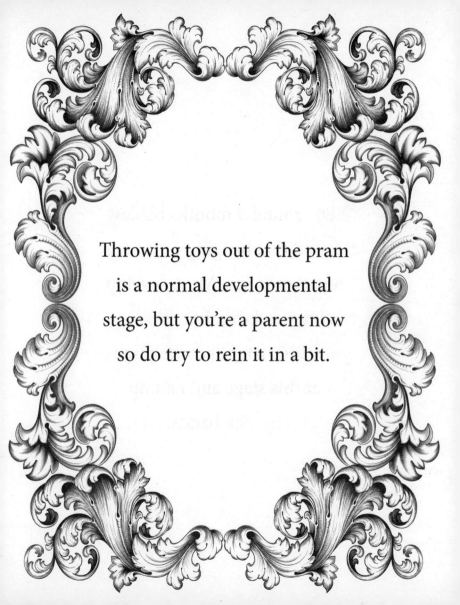

Throwing toys out of the pram
is a normal developmental
stage, but you're a parent now
so do try to rein it in a bit.

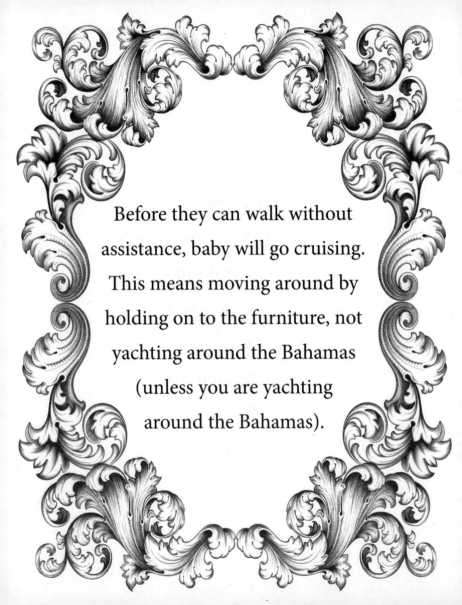

Before they can walk without assistance, baby will go cruising. This means moving around by holding on to the furniture, not yachting around the Bahamas (unless you are yachting around the Bahamas).

Around this time baby will be able to hold things in between their thumb and forefinger. This is known as the 'pincer grip', which will be vital for them when they're old enough to attend the sales.

At 10 months old, your baby

is as long as a pheasant.

As baby gets older, feeding time can become a battle of wills. But really Cook should be preparing the food you ask for, so don't settle for anything less.

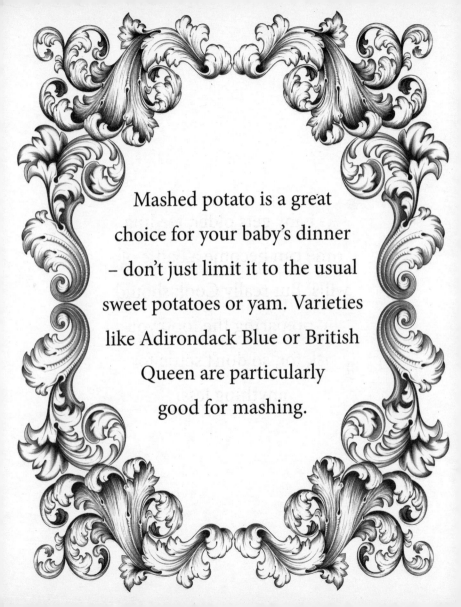

Mashed potato is a great choice for your baby's dinner – don't just limit it to the usual sweet potatoes or yam. Varieties like Adirondack Blue or British Queen are particularly good for mashing.

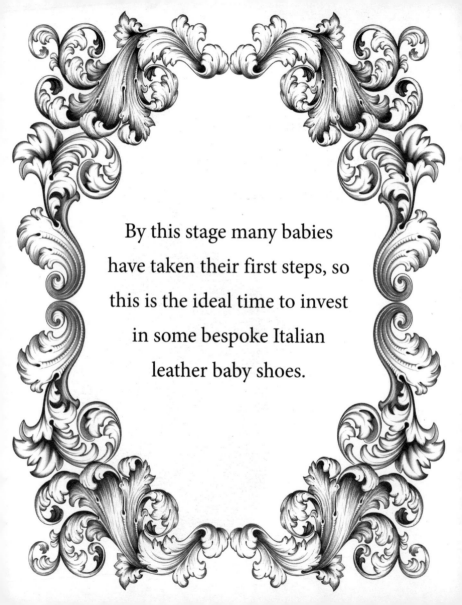

By this stage many babies
have taken their first steps, so
this is the ideal time to invest
in some bespoke Italian
leather baby shoes.

At 11 months old, your
baby weighs as much as
a *jamón ibérico*.

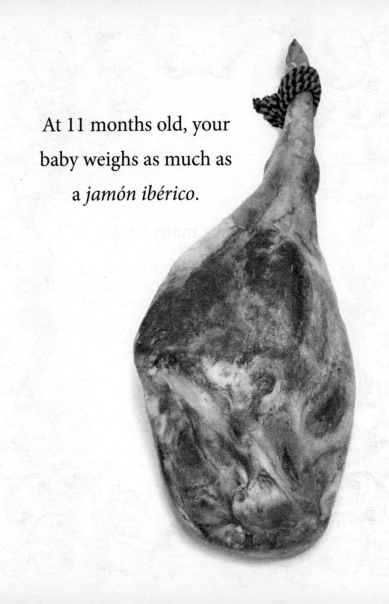

Storing things away in cupboards or neatly on shelves is a great way of keeping them out of baby's reach.

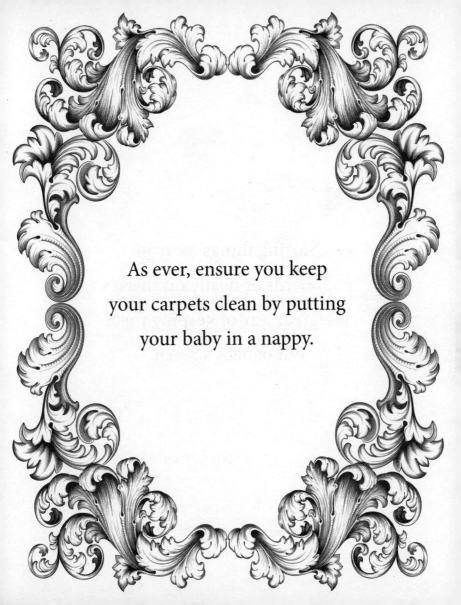

As ever, ensure you keep
your carpets clean by putting
your baby in a nappy.

At 12 months old, your
baby weighs as much as a
Pembroke Welsh Corgi.

# Baby's 1st Birthday

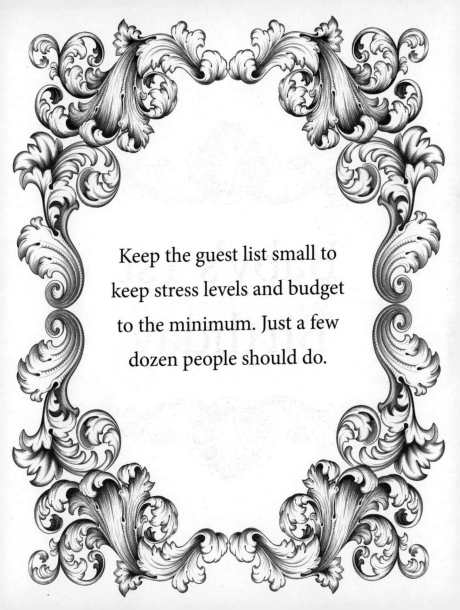

Keep the guest list small to keep stress levels and budget to the minimum. Just a few dozen people should do.

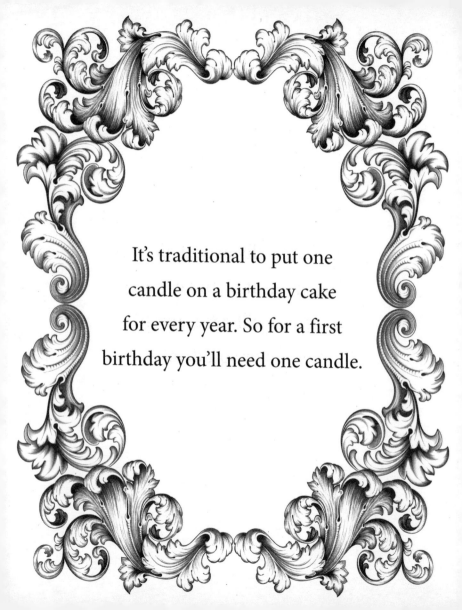

It's traditional to put one candle on a birthday cake for every year. So for a first birthday you'll need one candle.

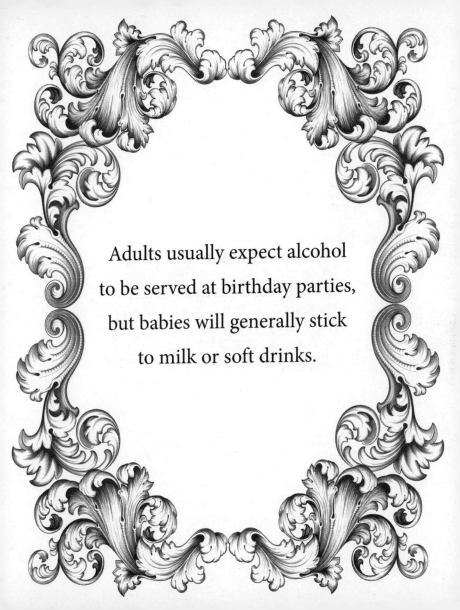

Adults usually expect alcohol
to be served at birthday parties,
but babies will generally stick
to milk or soft drinks.

A great gift for a baby is a mobile. Of course, an iPad will do the job just as well.

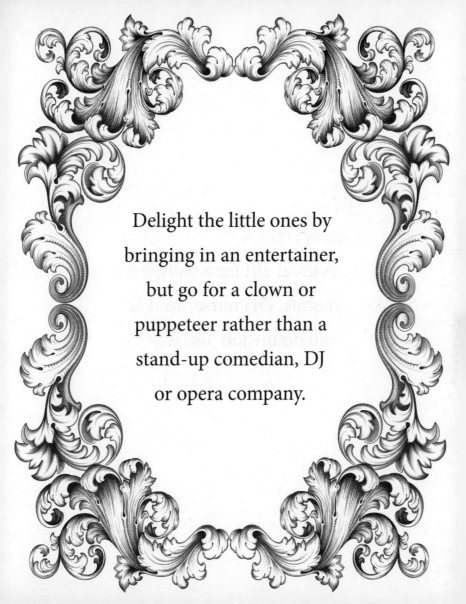

Delight the little ones by bringing in an entertainer, but go for a clown or puppeteer rather than a stand-up comedian, DJ or opera company.

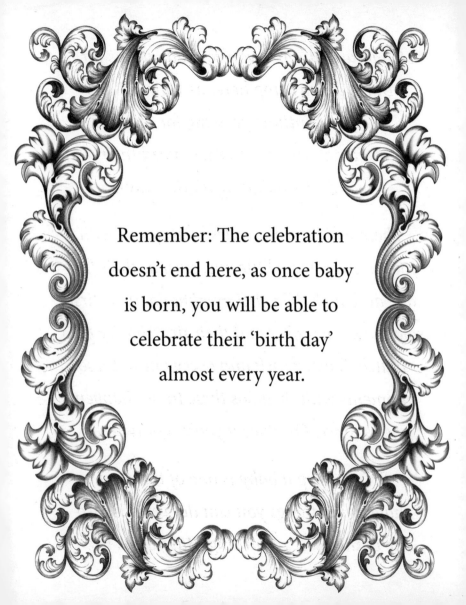

Remember: The celebration doesn't end here, as once baby is born, you will be able to celebrate their 'birth day' almost every year.

Congratulations – you've made it this far! But it doesn't stop here, as your child is likely to continue growing for another seventeen years (and will need their wardrobe updating all the way).

There will be many milestones ahead with your ever-growing little one, such as their first day at school, their first gymkhana, their first solo magazine cover and their first charity polo match. Savour each and every one of these moments with them, as these things happen only once. Or twice if you've got twins.

Bringing up a baby is one of the most challenging things you can do, yet it is also one of the most rewarding. But you've been *through the scariest bit now, and so sadly our paths must part. Still, though I may not be there with an expert tip for every occasion, rest assured I am with you in spirit.*

*And if the environmentally-minded of you are worried about what to do with this book now you've finished it, don't be. Why not gift it to a friend or loved one, or simply use it as a paperweight or a doorstop?*

*Whatever you choose to do with it, I hope you have found this little guide reassuring and enlightening, and that you and baby enjoy the delightful years to come as much as I shall enjoy the royalty statements.*

# Fin

# ACKNOWLEDGEMENTS

There are many people I'd like to thank – my friends, my family, my staff and my ghost-writers, who have asked if they can thank the following people too:

Jamie Coleman at Toby Eady Associates, our 'Creative Doula'; Kate Hewson, Henry Lord, Andrew Furlow and Stacey Croft (our perfect birthing partners); Johanna Herman; Freya Janes; Briana Janes; Rory and Nye O'Sullivan; Jamie East; Kate Faithfull-Williams; Juliet Stephens; Nico Bentley; Jayne Savva; the GTL SALGs for teaching us more about pregnancy and babies than books ever could; Bryony Gordon & baby Edie; Eos Chater; Lauren Geisler; Rowan Davies and all at Mumsnet Towers; Meri, James and Sebastian James Flash Sinclair-Smith.

(and not forgetting…)

Geraldine Azzopardi for her years of midwifery and paediatric nursing experience (and for giving birth and being the best Mum ever); Jules Azzopardi for instilling 37 years of bad jokes; Hannah Morrisroe for the inspiration; the Morrisroe sisters (Julie, Kezzer & Katie) for the tips and unending Chinese burns; Margaret Morrisroe for the child-rearing advice and the child-rearing of Mat; David Morrisroe for passing on the piss-taking gene.

# PICTURE ACKNOWLEDGEMENTS

### All images used under license from Shutterstock.com

1. Image Copyright Jiri Hera, 2013. / 2. Image Copyright Dasha Petrenko, 2013. / 3. Image Copyright Marilyn Barbone, 2013. / 4. Image Copyright Robyn Mackenzie, 2013. / 5. Image Copyright bonchan, 2013. / 6. Image Copyright Marilyn Barbone, 2013. / 7. Image Copyright Evgeny Karandaev, 2013. / 8. Image Copyright oriori, 2013. / 9. Image Copyright panda3800, 2013. / 10. Image Copyright Tsekhmister, 2013. / 11. Image Copyright kefiiir, 2013. / 12. Image Copyright Valentyn Volkov, 2013. / 13. Image Copyright Valentyn Volkov, 2013. / 14. Image Copyright Igor Sokolov, 2013. / 15. Image Copyright Elzbieta Sekowska, 2013. / 16. Image Copyright Kristina Pchelintseva, 2013. / 17. Image Copyright Volosina, 2013. /18. Image Copyright Jiang Hongyan, 2013. / 19. Image Copyright bonchan, 2013. / 20. Image Copyright Piotr Malczyk, 2013. / 21. Image Copyright Mark Studio, 2013 / 22. Image Copyright manfredxy, 2013 / 23. Image Copyright foodonwhite, 2013 / 24. Image Copyright Jiang Hongyan, 2013 / 25. Image Copyright picturepartners, 2013 / 26. Image Copyright gresei, 2013 / 27. Image Copyright design56, 2013 / 28. Image Copyright geniuscook_com, 2013 / 29. Image Copyright Aygul Bulte, 2013 / 30. Image Copyright unverdorben jr, 2013 / 31. Image Copyright Viktar Malyshchyts, 2013 / 32. Image Copyright MoonRaiter, 2013 / 33. Image Copyright Andi Berger, 2013 / 34. Image Copyright bonchan, 2013 / 35. Image Copyright Katrina Brown, 2013 / 36. Image Copyright Ermolaev Alexander, 2013 / 37. Image Copyright Tsekhmister, 2013 / 38. Image Copyright fuchi, 2013 / 39. Image Copyright schankz, 2013 / 40. Image Copyright ots-photo, 2013 / 41. Image Copyright P. Burghardt, 2013 / 42. Image Copyright O. Bellini, 2013 / 43. Image Copyright Irina oxilixo Danilova, 2013 / 44. Image Copyright Jiang Hongyang, 2013 / 45. Image Copyright Ekaterina V. Borisova, 2013 / 46. Image Copyright nito, 2013 / 47. Image Copyright Julia Remezova, 2013.

Frames copyright HiSunnySky, 2013.
Used under license from Shutterstock.com